AF593669

Shadows of Change

Photographs of a disappearing industrial landscape

For Carole
and for Lewis

SHADOWS *of* CHANGE

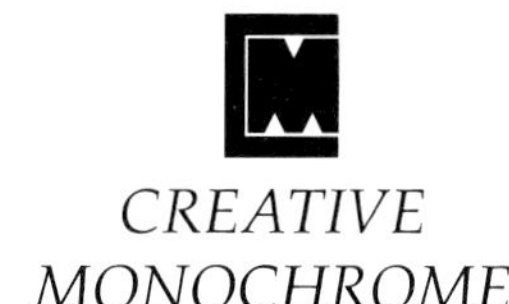

CREATIVE
MONOCHROME

SHADOWS OF CHANGE
Photographs of a disappearing industrial landscape
by Leigh Preston
with foreword by Graham Ovenden

Published in the UK by Creative Monochrome
20 St Peters Road, Croydon, Surrey, CR0 1HD.

British Library Cataloguing-in-Publication Data:
A catalogue record for this book is available
from the British Library

ISBN 1 873319 05 3
First edition, 1993

Printed in England by The Bath Press, Lower Bristol Road, Bath.

ACKNOWLEDGEMENTS
The author and publisher thank Davray Music Ltd and Carlin Music Corp for permission to quote a brief extract from *Return to Waterloo*, by Ray Davies, and Dukes Lodge Enterprises Ltd and Carlin Music Corp for permission to quote from *Hometown* by Witney Chapman. *Another Ticket*, words and music by Eric Clapton, copyright 1981 and 1993 by Eric Clapton, is reproduced by permission of Music Sales Ltd.

Leigh Preston wishes to thank the following people and organisations who have helped to make this book possible.

For encouragement and help: Ordnance Survey PS, Southampton CC, Solihull PS, The Royal Photographic Society;

Graham Ovenden, John Philpott, Bob Elliott, Jim Mansfield, Bob Moore, David Tann-Ailward, China Hamilton.

For friendship since we were kids: John Warwick and David Amery.

For all that was taught: David Skinner, Philip White and Ray Hadfield.

And lastly to Mother and Dad – for everything.

Contents

FOREWORD *7*
by Graham Ovenden

INTRODUCTION *9*

THE VIEW FROM OUR LAVATORY WINDOW *11*

CHASING SHADOWS *15*

PORTFOLIO *21*

TECHNICAL NOTES *109*

Foreword

Only incomprehension lays in wait for the artist who indulges in excessive personal analysis. This is particularly so when this narcissism leads to a belief that the ego alone (even if counter-pointed by autobiography) can hold meaning for a wider audience than self. For such individuals the specifically depicted remains the mere mechanics of man's ingenuity, but utterly fails to grasp the nature and poetry of the archetype. Unfortunately, most photographers masquerading as interpreters fall into this heresy – thus the general confusion and mediocrity of much 'photographic art'.

Leigh Preston is one of the chosen few: he possesses the ability to communicate autobiography, intensified through the 'Blakeian Crystal', and in doing so makes concrete a sense of personal wonder. He lays before us images which are more than specific portraits of place: he also imbues them with an authentic mood and poetry.

One hardly needs to dwell on Preston's technical proficiency, as the images presented here are strong in structure as in substance. This artist is also a master of light and darkness – I do not use the word 'shade', for the intense velvet blacks in his imagery are fraught with speculation. Preston understands perfectly the true nature of the photographic medium, how form grows from or is lost into the void of our imaginings.

His images depict past industry, modest homes, and decaying, angled structures whose substance is softened by time and organic growth: this is not dissimilar in sentiment to that great recurring theme of western art – the works of man (whether it be broken antiquity or the industrial revolution) encroached on by nature. How often the fragments of an age or life can be more compelling to our sensibilities than the perfect whole. I do not think that these observations lead to sentimentality or an excessive nostalgia; no, more an awareness of past humanities which have shaped and pervaded the atmosphere of an environment.

Any danger that Leigh Preston's images might fall into visual seduction are strongly countered by his understanding of the graphic angularity of design. Even so, he is aware that the brittle geometry of a broken window or the arbitrary shaping of a water-filled pot-hole can act as a reflector of light. Thus this mirror may be radiant or act as the medium in which we may see as "through a glass darkly": our imaginings are led to both negative and positive speculation.

There is an intensity in Preston's vision which reminds me of Thomas Burke's *Limehouse Nights*. Though, whereas Burke brings into sharp relief the humble players of his invention, in Preston one is left to sense the shadows of those who inhabited and worked within the structures held by the photographer's alchemy. It is an ability, indeed, which enables this artist to create images which are at once both austere and yet laden with a sense of human association.

As our industrial heritage recedes into the certain past and our uncertain future looms ever darker, there is a danger we might come to view such monuments only by the positive light of day, so dismissing the imagery of the "dark Satanic mills" to little-read social histories. I think not, if we see – as does Preston – both with criticism and affection. For these structures and artefacts of past endeavour will be observed, as all things made must eventually be:

> "And because time in itself ... can receive no alteration, the hallowing ... must consist in the shape or countenance which we put upon the affaires that are incident in these days." *(Richard Hooker)*

Graham Ovenden
December 1992

Introduction

Standing in the middle of nowhere
Wondering where to begin
Caught between tomorrow and yesterday
Between now and then

Ray Davies

This book is a journey back home. It is an attempt to try to catch what I let go by: a pictorial way of showing affection and respect for the backdrop to my childhood. I knew this environment as everyday, like a friend, a world my grandmother showed me just by living there.

The photographs are coupled to the unreal curved mirror that the mind's eye gives to yesterday. I went searching among the pride etched out in rust and sunlight for what's gone and cannot be replaced, trying to make up the distance between now and then. So much has been chiselled away. It's easy to be seduced by the romance of decay, pulled by the broken and discarded to the era of ghost-eyed warehouses, the files of kerbstones and sooty cobbles, frowning terraces and a collage of mills and railway viaducts.

These pictures are raw and simple, with abrupt angles and an emotion pulled down from cloud and sky. Colour has been replaced by silvers and greys, by dark and light, by echoes and shadows, providing a more solemn gallery to industrial settings.

I have not compensated for what it was like to survive and work in such surroundings, and although I'm aware of the dirty, mean, chilly vice of the 1930s, I've only viewed these scenes romantically, not factually.

My grandmother lived in such a situation, as did my mother. These words and pictures represent part of their legacy, subconsciously given; a reminder of when life was harsher, but less hectic, and less biased towards material things. Times change but the bond remains, all part of the person I am.

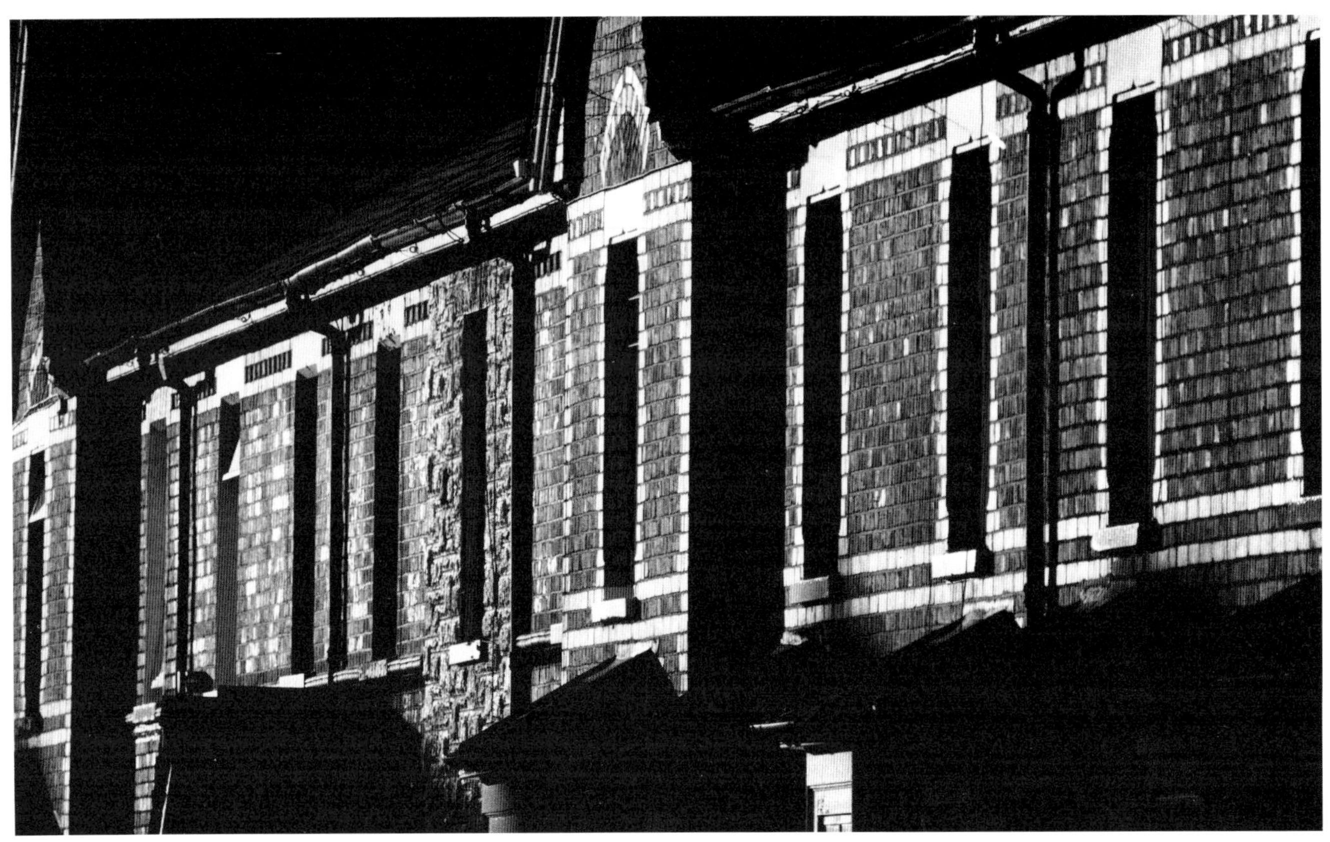

Terraced houses, Reading
Formative impressions

Grass is gone
There's only concrete to walk upon
The motorway has been through and gone
There's nothing here left to see

Hometown. Everything has been changed around
Buildings so high, you can't even spy
The sun going down

Witney Chapman

The view from our lavatory window

In a sense, these pictures are nearly all in one place. In reality, I travelled all over Britain to take them. Mostly, I drew my inspiration from what I grew up with, that just happened to be in Reading. It could have been anywhere.

A lot more time was spent looking outwards in those days. Today people look inwards at the TV, just to look out. Yellow lace curtains don't twitch so much now; the view from the car is in no way compensation for that from a railway carriage window.

I used to watch the setting sun from our lavatory window. We lived on a hill then, and by standing on the loo seat, I could see a grey skyline of terraces, church spires, factory chimneys, all subdued by a smudgy, smokey atmosphere; the window on my world.

I watched the world go by with an innocence I don't have any more, seeing it all wide-eyed as a little boy, untouched by the social implications of the grey silhouette I looked out upon. Happy endless days, climbing trees, running with friends, playing football, and the usual antics. Favourite, in terrace streets, was shoving paraffin-soaked rags up cast iron drainpipes and setting them alight – they made a really good howling noise, especially if you got four or five going at once. We used to wrap dog turds in newspaper, setting light to the parcel on some poor soul's doorstep. Knock the knocker. Out they came, in carpet slippers and stamped on it: spectacular it was.

We reserved our best pranks for those people we didn't like. Even now I smile to think of the mustard and cress we posted through letter-boxes, and then watered it. Getting caught meant a certain 'thick ear', but who wants to be angelic all the time? We used to turn halfpennies into pennies by putting them on the railway lines, or supplement pocket money by pressing 'button B'.

The characters in the streets were different then. More people wore hats, and gaberdine; leather shopping bags were much in vogue. Much talk was carried on over fences or on allotments.

I remember uncles, moulded differently from uncles these days. They hid all day behind newspapers. When they smoked they were invisible. Sometimes they disappeared into damp dark sheds, rummaging in old 'baccy' tins for oily screws and hinges to mend things. Aunties took you on bus trips or off to Sunday School, hair pasted down with Brylcream, convinced that a week's errant behaviour could be made up for by an hour's religious fidgeting.

Grannies were always white-haired and benevolent, except to insurance men or to neighbours who accidentally creosoted their lupins. We ran their errands, rode with them on trolley buses, fetched their coal – have you ever wondered where all the tom-cats sleep now since the demise of the coal bunker? We bought new gas mantles for them: grannies were not keen on "the electric", and viewed it with deep mistrust, not believing it could ever flow any way but downhill!

Then there was the outside loo, with a wooden life-raft for a seat, the hissing cistern, proudly embossed with *Armitage* or *Twyford* or some such legend, and torn newspaper. That one day all this would vanish and disappear entered no one's head.

White cats used to sun themselves on grimy walls, eyeing next door's aviary with a mixture of glee and suspicion; they all had distinguished names like Tiddles or Chesney.

Washed shirts used to hang surrendering on back garden lines, hoisted like sails by elaborate pulley systems and kept aloft by wooden clothes props. The props used to break occasionally when being employed for purposes other than 'propping', such as pole-vaulting across cold frames or across the rhubarb condemned to spend its life forcing its way through rusty-eyed buckets.

People had more bonfires; old codgers used to light them and pile them high with grass cuttings, suggesting Red Indian ancestry, upsetting mother on wash day. I well remember someone in our road getting her sooty washing analysed by some chap in a white coat from Earley Power Station. Back he came, "Well, madam, there's two types of soot: round soot and square soot. This is square soot, ours is round – blame the railway!"

The power station chimneys were visible for miles around, the everyday view. Maybe this is why I include chimneys in so many pictures. Trains were steam, going to Bristol or South Wales, maybe the West Country. The shunting of coal wagons went on well into the night, an accepted background noise.

Not many people had cars then, but the Bath Road was always busy with lorries. I mainly remember Wolseleys, Morris Oxfords and Ford Prefects in our road. The memories are not so much of the cars themselves, but of letting-down tyres and fixing balloons to the exhausts. We had an Austin 7 for a while. Those were the days when the Aldermaston Marches would stop the traffic along the Bath Road: thousands of people and banners, and yet nobody in power really listened, even then.

To amuse ourselves we made highly suspect modes of conveyance – you can't get the pram wheels today. Another example of our quest for speed was racing down the old quarry slope, totally out of control on sheets of tattered corrugated iron – there were still a lot of 'Just Williams' about then. Those days had more gold in them; an ocean of hours that was childhood.

The TV hardly featured in our lives. My other grandmother, who didn't share the same mistrust of electricity, and being better off, had an *EKCO* 14". It took a good ten minutes to warm up. Later, we had a *Pye*, that used to glow in the corner. We watched, fascinated, programmes like *Mr Pastry, Hiram Halliday, The Vital Spark, Harry Worth* and *Michael Bentine's Square World.*

Machines were rare. We possessed a radiogram, an exceptionally noisy Hoover that scared the budgie, and a washing-machine that used to try to emigrate next door when mother wasn't looking. That was life as it was, I only wish I had photographs to go with it all.

It was necessary to go to school. We were conveyed there by a Mr Perkins, driving a green and cream Bedford Duple, that rattled and shook while we sang Beatles songs at the back. This was 1963 – the days (or, rather, nights) of radio static, listening under the sheets to Luxembourg 208. Merseyside legends. Charlton scoring goals. Barrington and Edrich making high scores at cricket.

As I say, all this was tempered by the need to go to school. It terrified me: massive brick buildings with bells tolling, big frowning windows, green and white painted bricks inside, wooden ink-stained desks. Everything seemed so dark.

Primary school days were not something I remember at all fondly. All was controlled either by the stern, grey-suited headmaster with a menacing bark, disciplinarian and rigid, or by "Grumpy", the brown-overalled caretaker. His job seemed to revolve round the boilerhouse; that and mending goalposts.

We had other equally dominant characters. A dinner lady whose eyes were so far apart she could see down her ears. Prefects, school bullies, milk monitors, niffy plimsoles, the 'three Rs', conkers and black eyes all played their part in early school life. There were disasters, like the school nativity play when someone was ill inside the donkey costume or school sports day with such dangerous events as the sack race – you could easily break your nose falling over. I'd like to draw a veil over school dinners – no fond memories there.

We had some fun climbing on the roof to retrieve tennis balls and getting rescued. And I still smile at Mr Jenkins' attempt to get eleven boys to an away cricket match in a Messerschmidt Bubble Car, three at a time! Assembly could be disrupted by singing one line behind everyone else while Miss Barnes thumped out *O God our help in ages past* on the old rosewood upright. I wonder what happened to the small boy I once was?

What I miss today is the character and the permanence of that world modelled in brick – long since sacrificed for roads and enterprise zones. The view beyond the window changed. England got pulled down, in more ways than one.

Chasing shadows

Paper-round money gave me freedom to travel, even if I was only eleven and still in short trousers! Often it was to London, but I also had my first glimpse of the North and the dialogue 'tween town and moorland – all seen from a railway carriage. Sheffield, Liverpool, Manchester, Glasgow, Newcastle, the 'people's republic of Doncaster' – by the time I was fifteen, I'd travelled to them all, getting a feeling for those northern skylines that never left me and later re-emerged in pictures, first as paintings, then as photographs. My art master, Philip White, taught me about shape and pattern, and he taught me about light. He helped me to see.

In 1972, I left home to work in Munich during the Olympic Games. I recall the warmth of that summer and the friendliness of the village. And then how cold it became when the terrorists tore it all apart with bullets. After hitch-hiking around Europe, I moved to Southampton, working for the Ordnance Survey. Reading changed, but I only want to remember it as it was.

It was not until 1977 that I bought my first camera, a secondhand Canon FTB. With the purchase of that camera, photography became an obsession. My time away from work was spent travelling or among the mountains, away from the pace of life. Landscape was my real interest, working only in colour. Large chunks of my salary and leave went on travelling to take pictures, with the hope of selling them later. Arizona, Utah, California, and on other occasions, Minnesota, the mid-West and Wyoming; seeing what I once only dreamed of. Vast open spaces, the isolation and loneliness, deserts, canyons, prairie: such natural beauty all should see, and man should leave alone. Australia, visited later on, inspired similar moods.

The pictures I took in black and white had to be nostalgic. I tried to make them belong to a period long since departed: turning the page back. Although David Skinner, a teacher at my secondary school in Reading, had taught me basic darkroom techniques, it wasn't until 1983 that I made my first 'proper' monochrome print. That picture was of the P & O liner *Canberra*, taken at night in the Western Docks at Southampton. In some ways it recalls early visits in the mid-60s when Dad took us to see the Cunard Queens depart. When those liners set course across the Atlantic for the last time, Southampton began to die as a port; its glamour faded, its tall cranes stood silent.

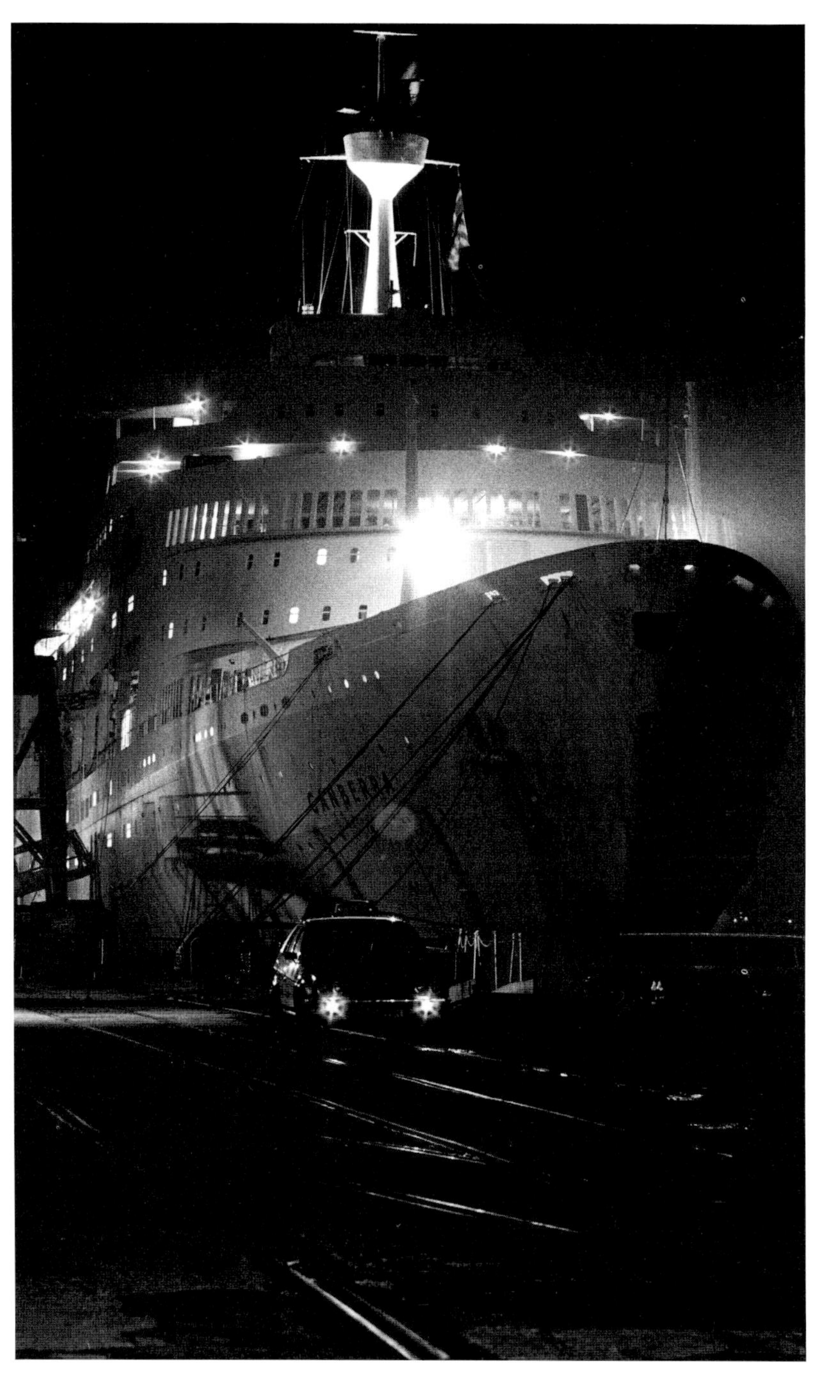

SS Canberra, Western Docks, Southampton

"My first 'proper' monochrome print"

The pictures in the following portfolio are nearly all from Britain. This is a more complete story than my shots of Australia and the States. Lowry and Bill Brandt are major influences, as are the painter, Atkinson Grimshaw, Ealing films and *Picture Post*. I drew some inspiration from J B Priestley's *English Journey* too.

The first 'shadow of change' I photographed was in Clitheroe, Lancashire, sparking off a linked series that became the backbone of my work. For almost ten years I collected negatives in such places as Accrington, Wigan, Burnley, Rochdale and Halifax – returning to what I'd seen from the train years before. These were sad, economically limping towns, laid waste by closure and redundancy, tired and worn down by a hard life, condemned by time, bruised by authoritarian vandalism and political indifference. Nobody cared about the old order of architecture and the echoing loneliness of old quaysides in Liverpool. There was no respect for the stark industrial settings of Oldham, with its closed mill gates and cobbles. That's why I photographed them: to pay my respects and to record their unique character. That era is over and cannot be mothballed. For me, Britain today stands for nothing but an eclipsed past: too many listened to the hollow promises.

There was a lighter side to all this. I found it in the accented conversations of the faded characters I met. Once, in a pub in Bacup, noticing I was startled by the lion's head next to the bar, the landlord offered, "Don't mind 'im, lad, he's dead".

I tried taking a self-portrait on the M6 once. It was at Junction 22, where the exit sign bears both my names. A passing motorised constable felt that what I was engaged in "doesn't actually constitute an emergency, sir"!

The grumbling was funny too. "Canal's overflowed and inundated me brussels". Or, "I 'ad horse in 2.30 at Haydock"; neighbour, with cloth cap, vest and stubble, "Did it win?"; "Oh aye, nearly won t'3 o'clock!".

Or there was the landlady (who assured me she'd put on weight since she gave up wrestling!) of one of the many guest houses I frequented on my photographic travels. She was very apologetic at breakfast one morning: "Sorry yer eggs av' come hard boiled, lad, but I usually time them by traffic lights I can see from kitchen window. They've packed up working and yon copper's got no bloody idea of what three and a half minutes is!"

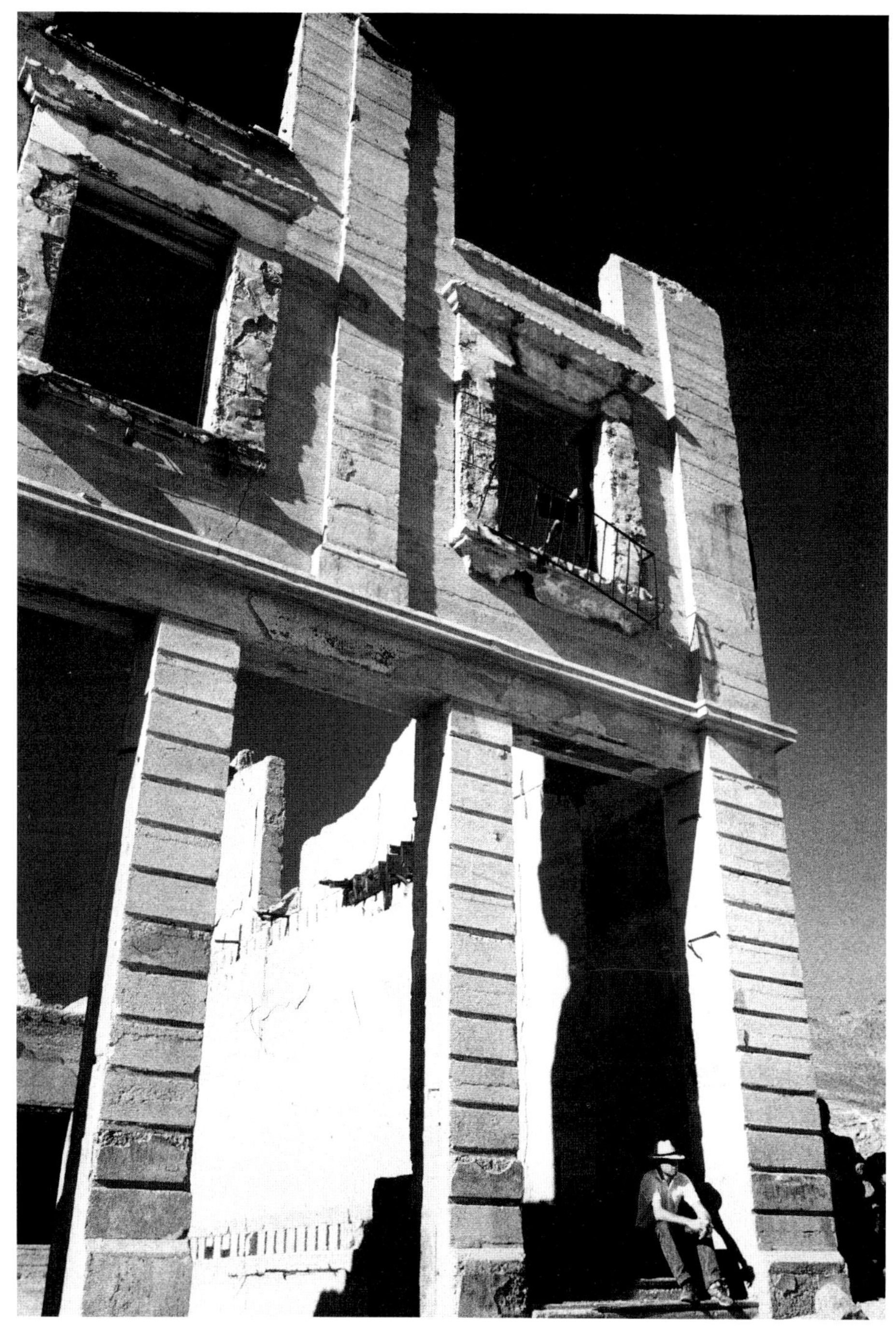

Derelict bank building, Rhyolite, Nevada
Self-portrait

It has to be said I've stayed in some pretty seedy boarding houses. In Leeds one time, the fried bread had the hard moral edge of suspicion because I was in late the previous night.

I found a note pinned on a loo door, "Cleaner, please leave an extra roll tomorrow". Good hotel that. In some places the lights go out when you change TV channels. And then there are those establishments with sloping floors and wardrobe doors that open voluntarily as soon as you get into bed. Some have sash windows, jammed open, directly in line with the prevailing weather. And then there's the bath – white with green stains and an immovable wire basket containing a yellow plastic duck, a cracked bar of coal tar soap, someone else's flannel and, if you are lucky, a hairless scrubbing brush!

It holds a magnetic attraction for me, seediness. Finding my pictures below railway arches or derelict mills in Stockport, looking for clues to unlock the past along the Manchester Ship Canal, using gnarled old fence posts as foregrounds. Anything that belongs to that era grabs my attention – cast iron lamp-posts, old telephone boxes, abandoned cars – a story from remnants is all I can tell. Like the shadows on warehouse walls in Bermondsey.

The photographs I have of London are like a diary, but a diary with too many pages missing. So much has been torn away – Wapping, Shadwell, Limehouse, Stepney: all overtaken by the turning tide called 'progress'. It is as if the big City men are frightened of the patina of grime or the working city landscape detracting from the uncompromising towers of windows which look down upon the East End.

The Royal Docks, where in the late '50s and early '60s the lifeblood of a nation flowed, are now unbelievably desolate. Pride, like the economy, has deserted the Thames and the dockland community that served her. London has been auctioned off to the highest bidder, and the East End people are left behind to think on what happened to this city that its people once loved.

Men fought hard for a wage in such places – the weed-choked skeleton of Consett, Swindon's abandoned railway works: places of pride and craftsmen. The silence rings loud in the shipyards of Clydebank, Cammell Laird's and on the Tyne. What future for the unturning pithead wheels in the Rhondda or for the collieries of East Durham, such as Vane Tempest and Easington?

The coal pickers are still here; the wind smells of coal, and the North Sea is tainted black – much the same as the economic prospects of these areas. This too is part of Britain, an isolated home to hopeless aspirations, the menace of loan sharks and life on 'the assistance'. Few politicians will walk here to witness the wreckage they make of other people's lives.

The wind of change is blowing again, bringing anger and hurt, symptoms of the arrogant granite face of economics. What the property developers and money men have done to Britain for short-lived gain appals me. Concrete and grey high rise have changed whole communities and cut the thread of harmony that once thrived.

Values have shifted to self and greed. It's painful to see people's meek ambition and impotent fury on empty factory walls: "Guy Fawkes, where are you, now that we need you?"

These pictures are of places and everyday things that mattered to me, as I prefer to remember them, sometime other than now. Precious moments disturbed only by the future. I travelled far and wide to capture these photographs, trying to find a little of what I saw years ago. Always there was something else to see before it finally disappeared, always another ticket to buy. It has taken ten years, and I've ended up with nothing but a feint shadow of how it once was: a shadow of change.

My father's interest in photography kept me enthusiastic; the emotion came from my mother. Once she said to me, "Do it now son, because now is the only moment you get". I photographed these places while there was still time.

Portfolio

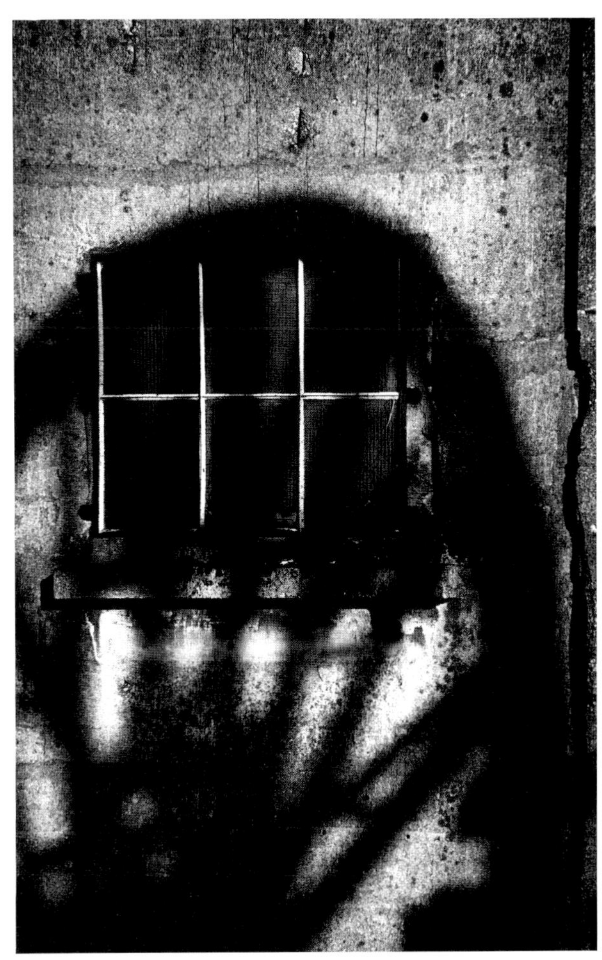

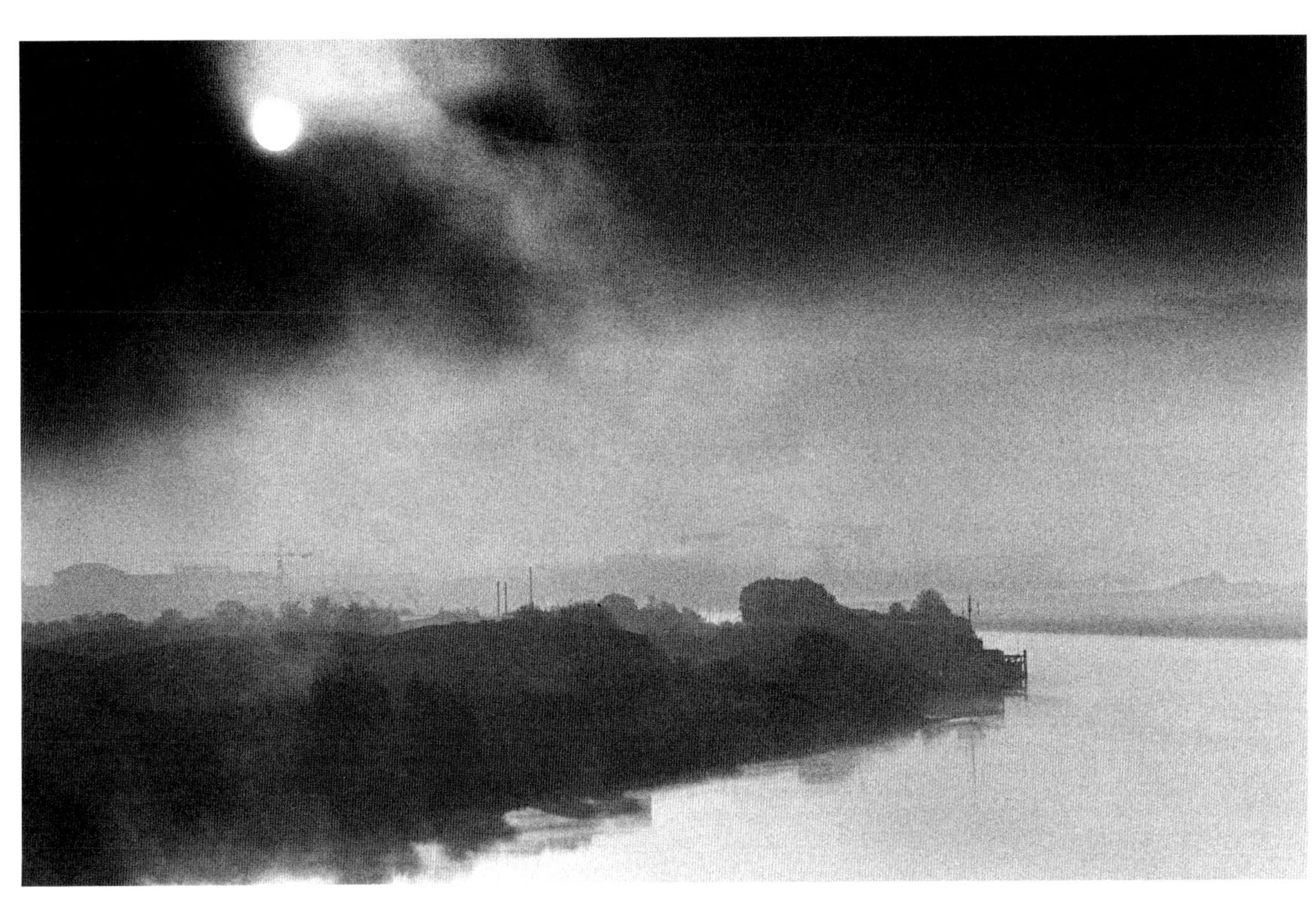

Sunrise, looking towards Clydebank

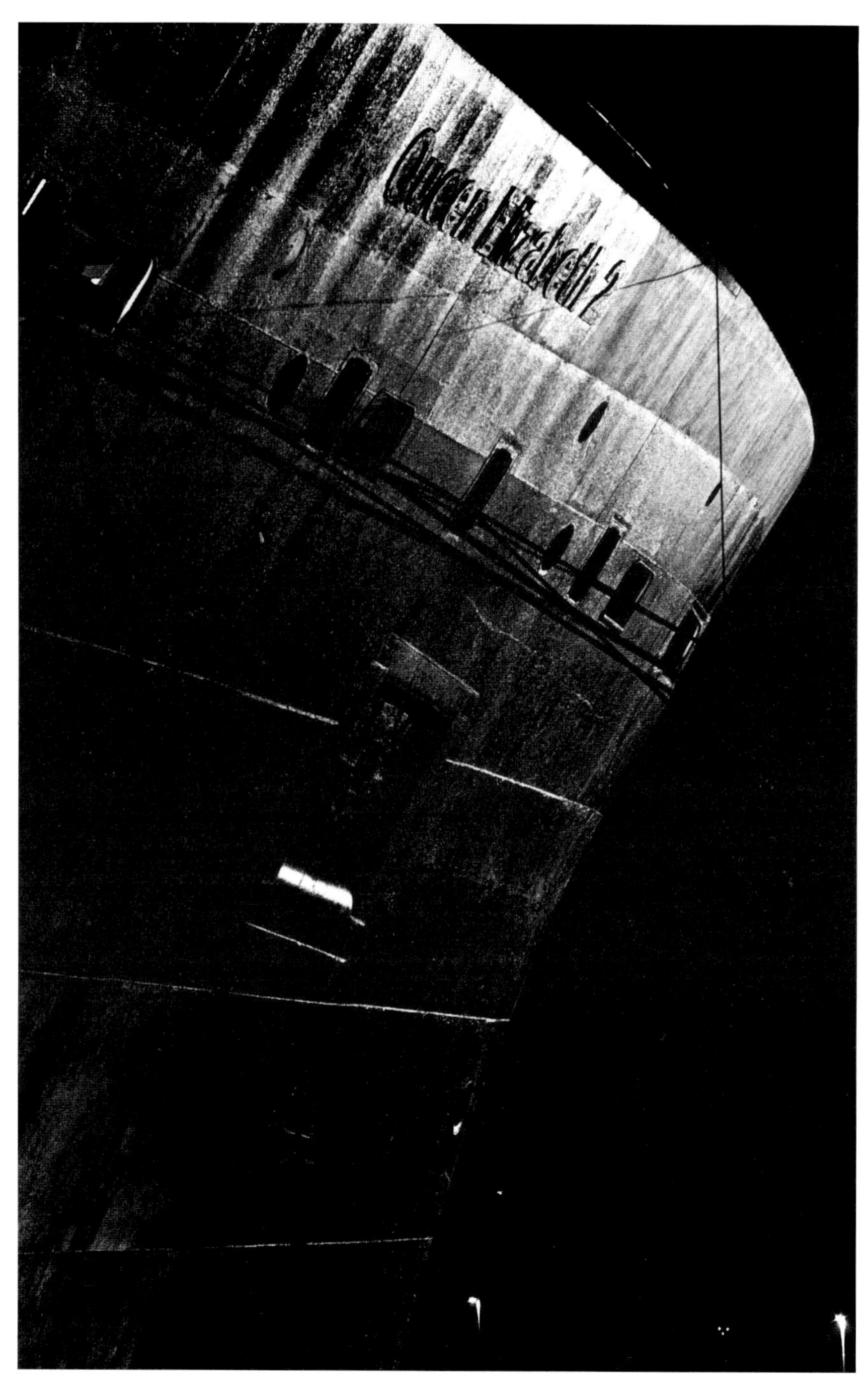

Queen Elizabeth II
Southampton

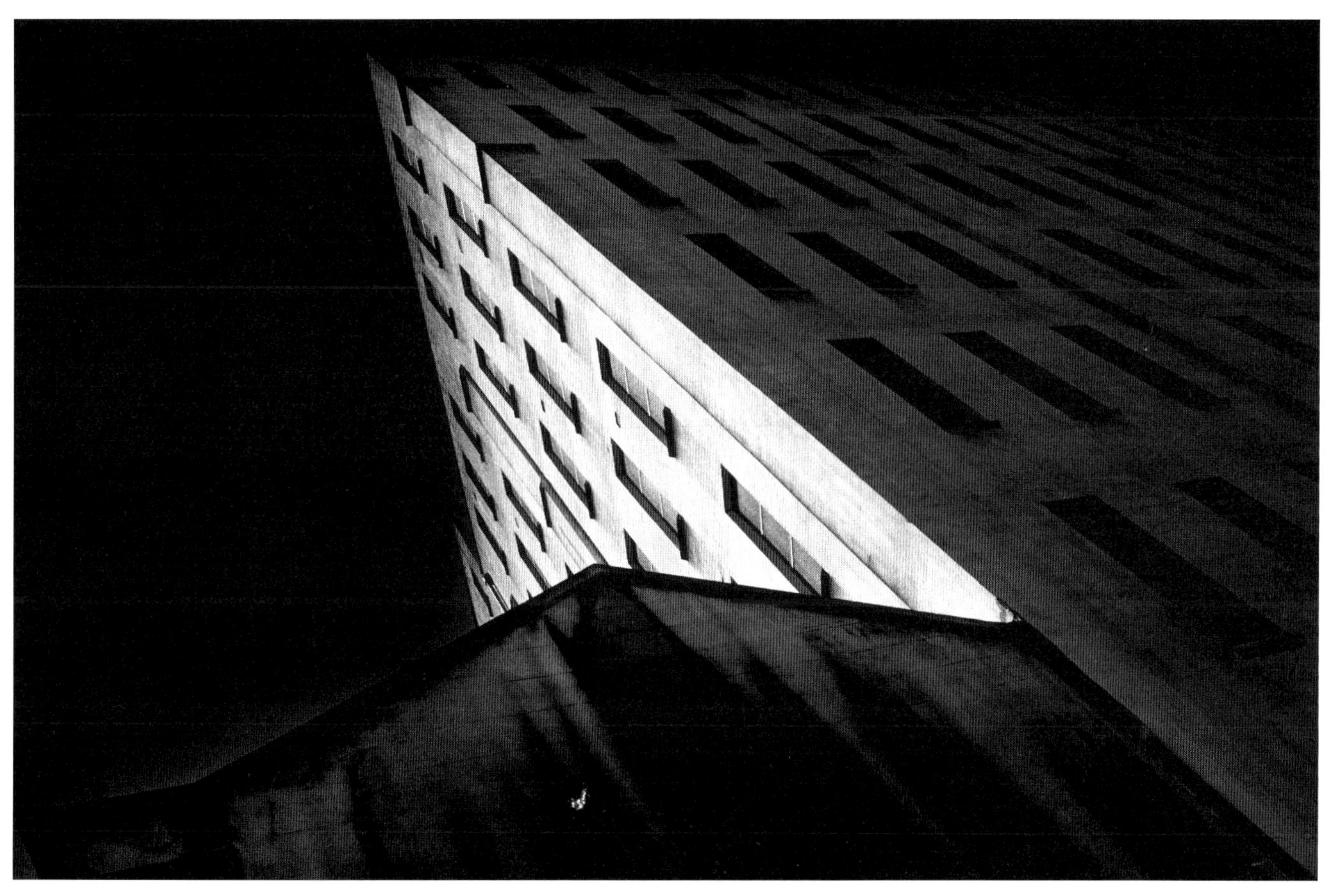

Tobacco warehouse
Bristol

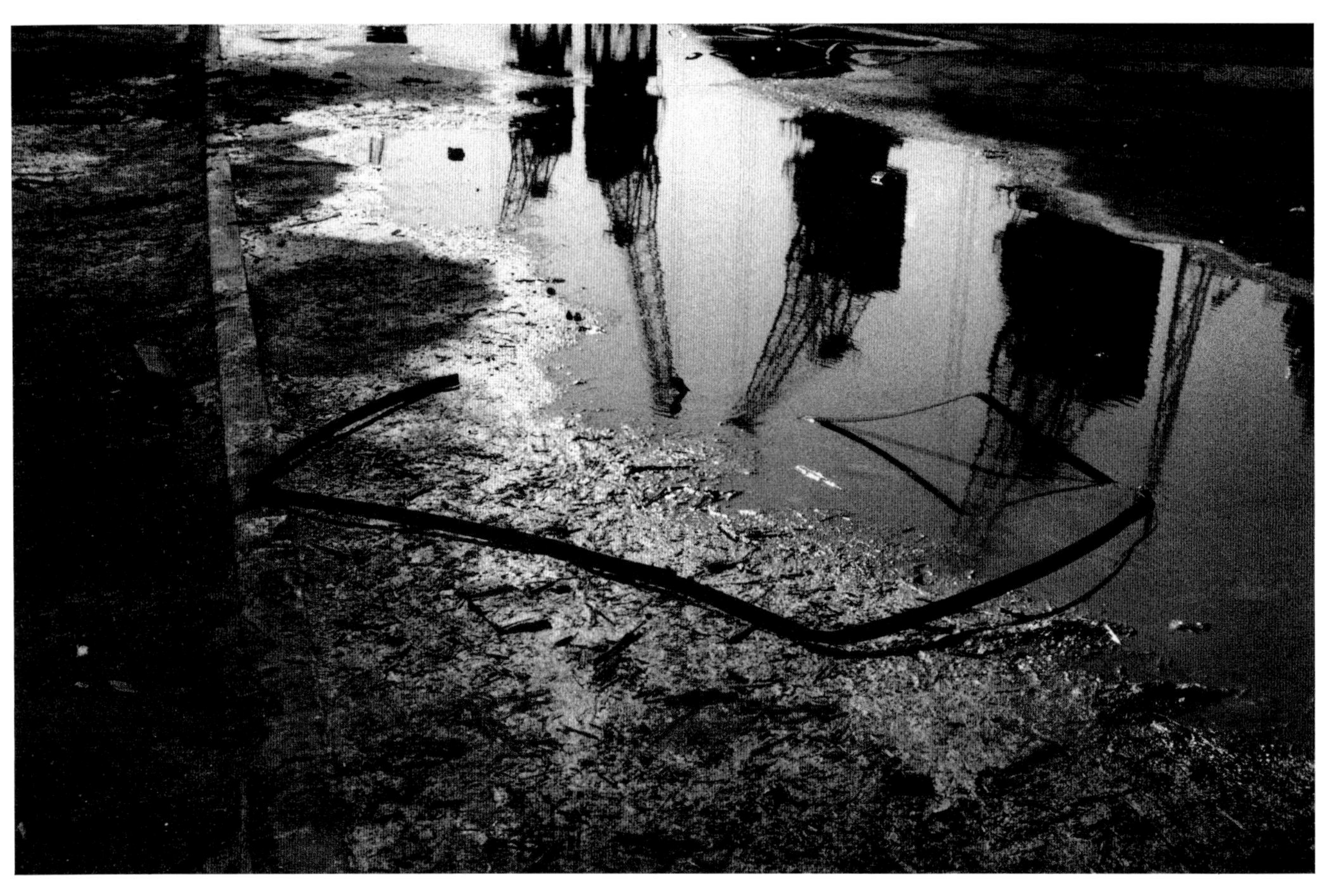

Newport, South Wales

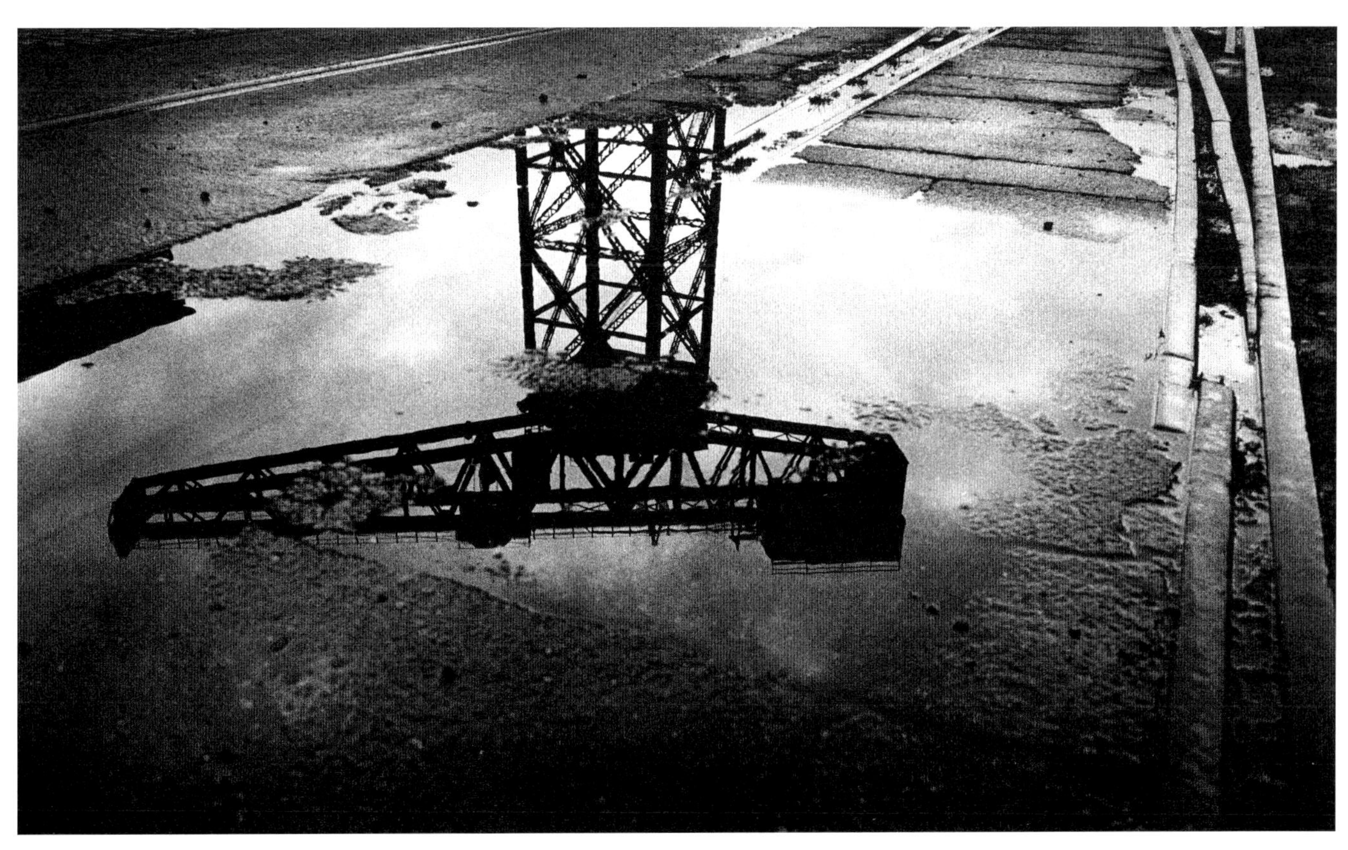

Clydeside

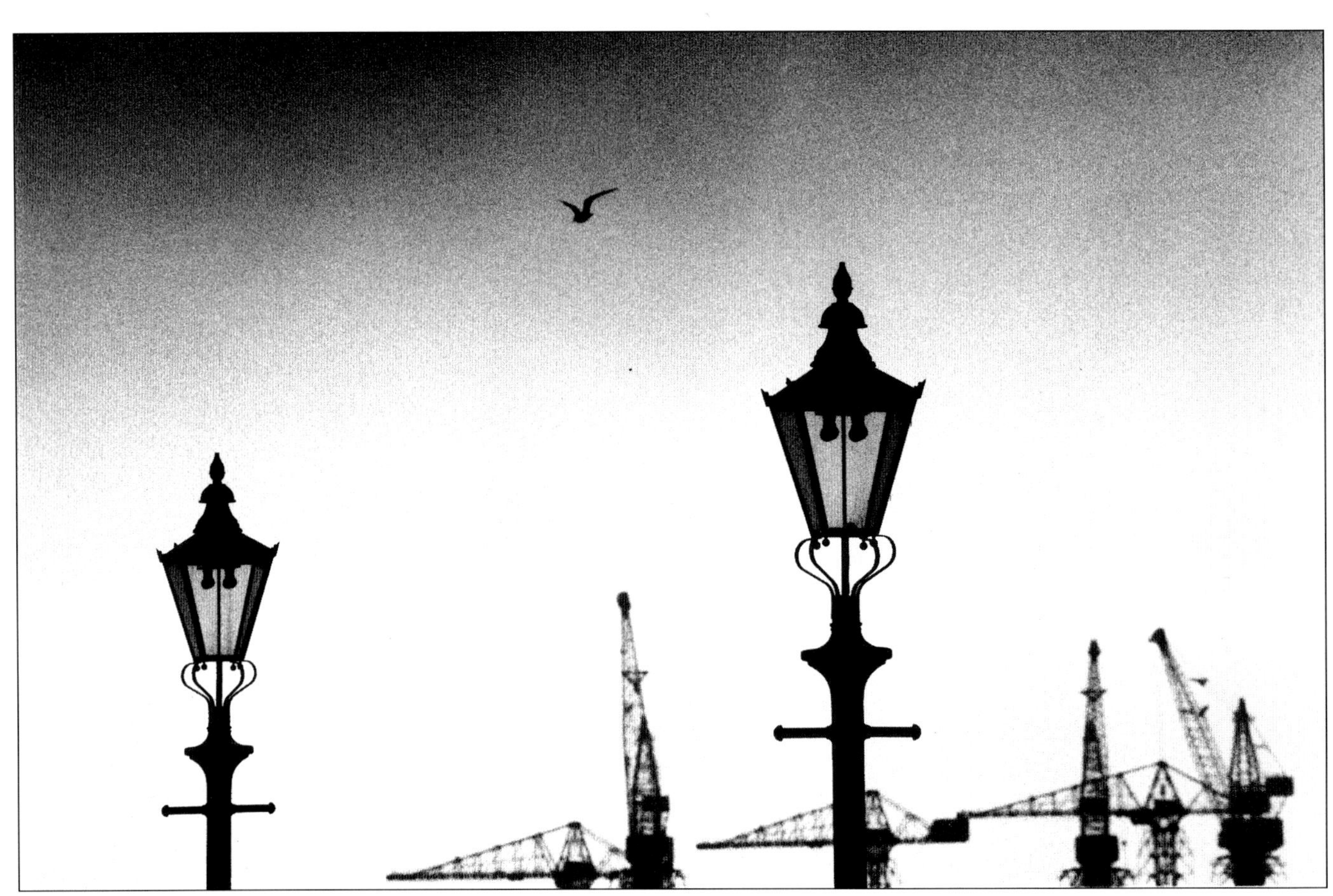

Birkenhead skyline

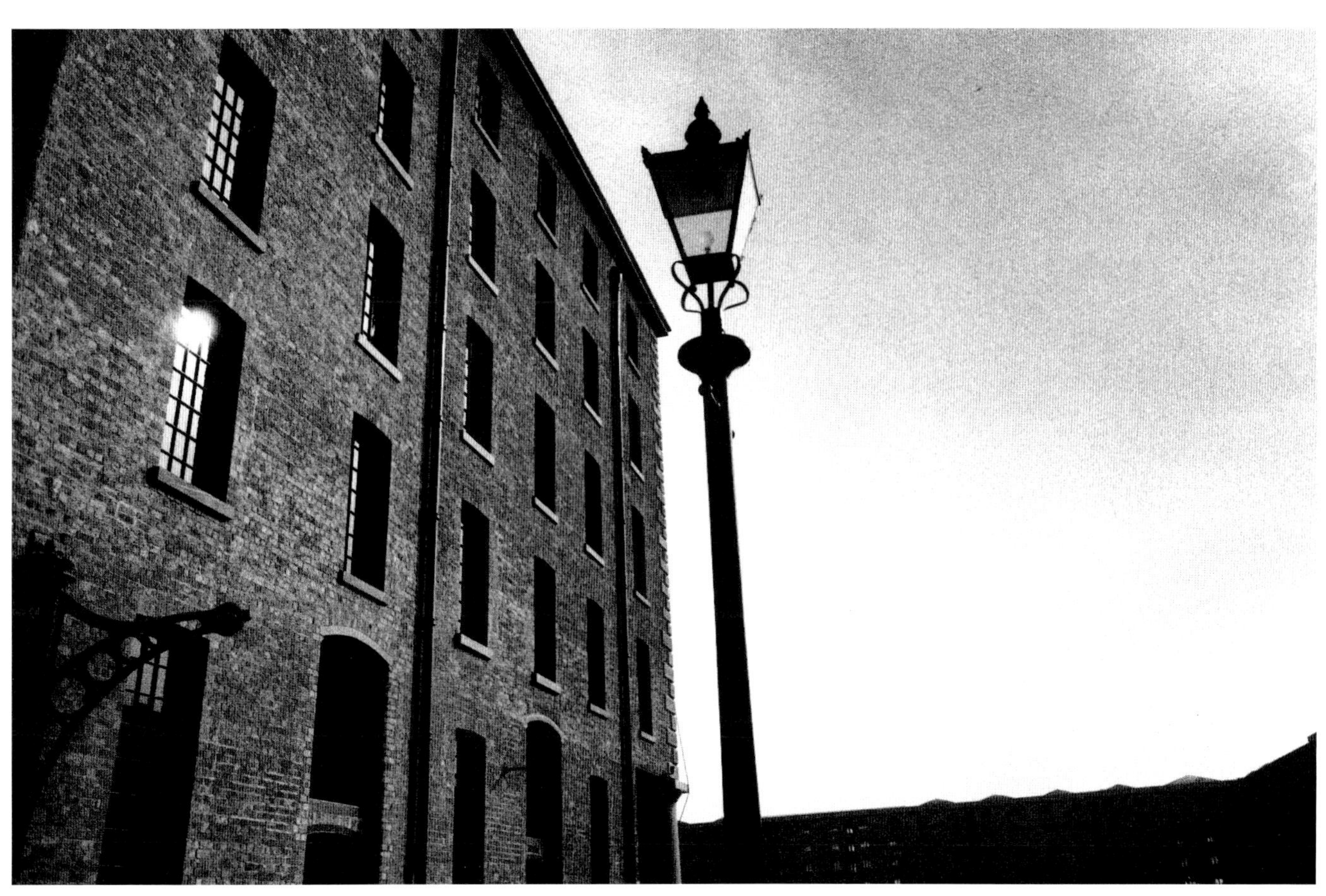

Albert Dock, Liverpool

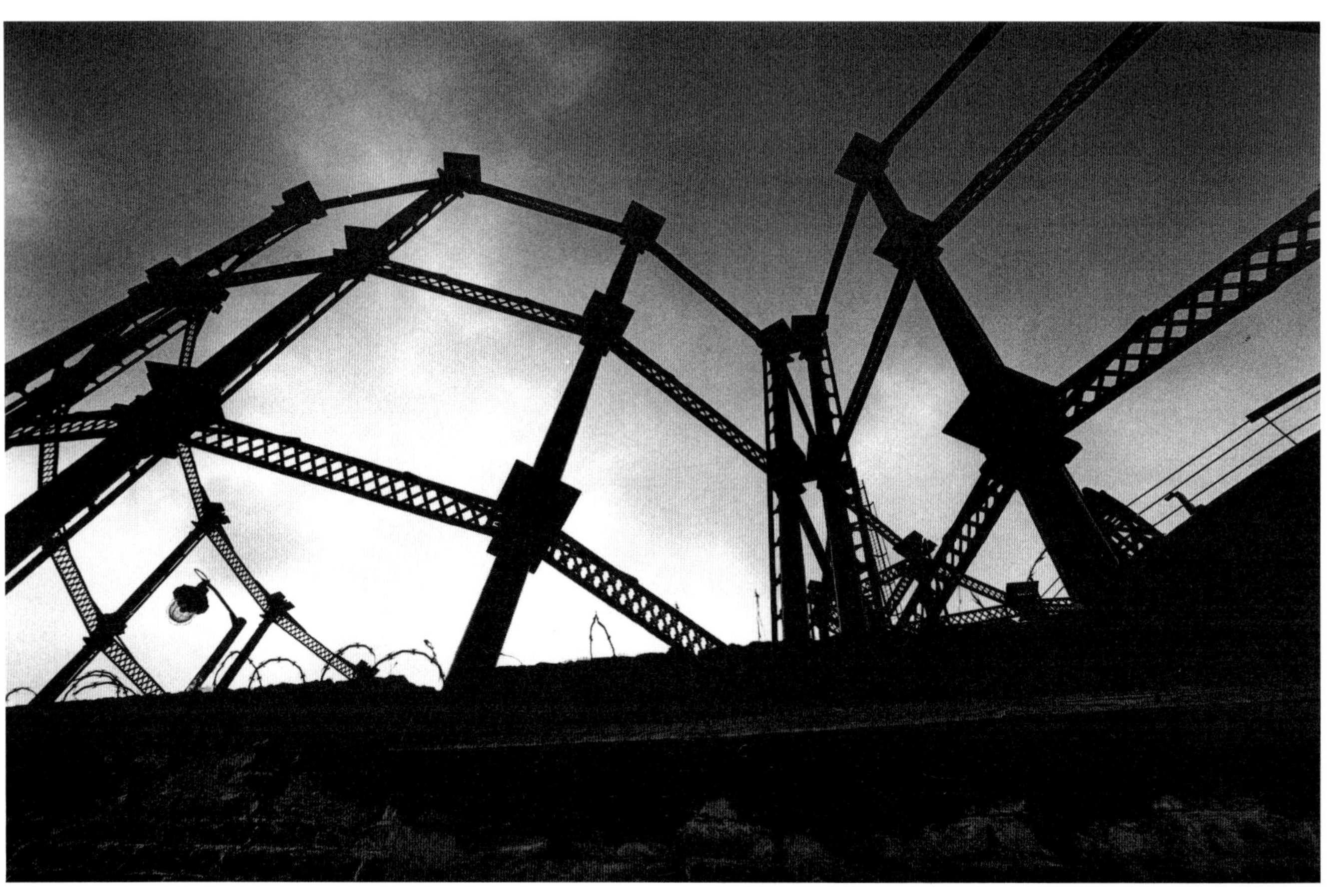

Gasworks, North London

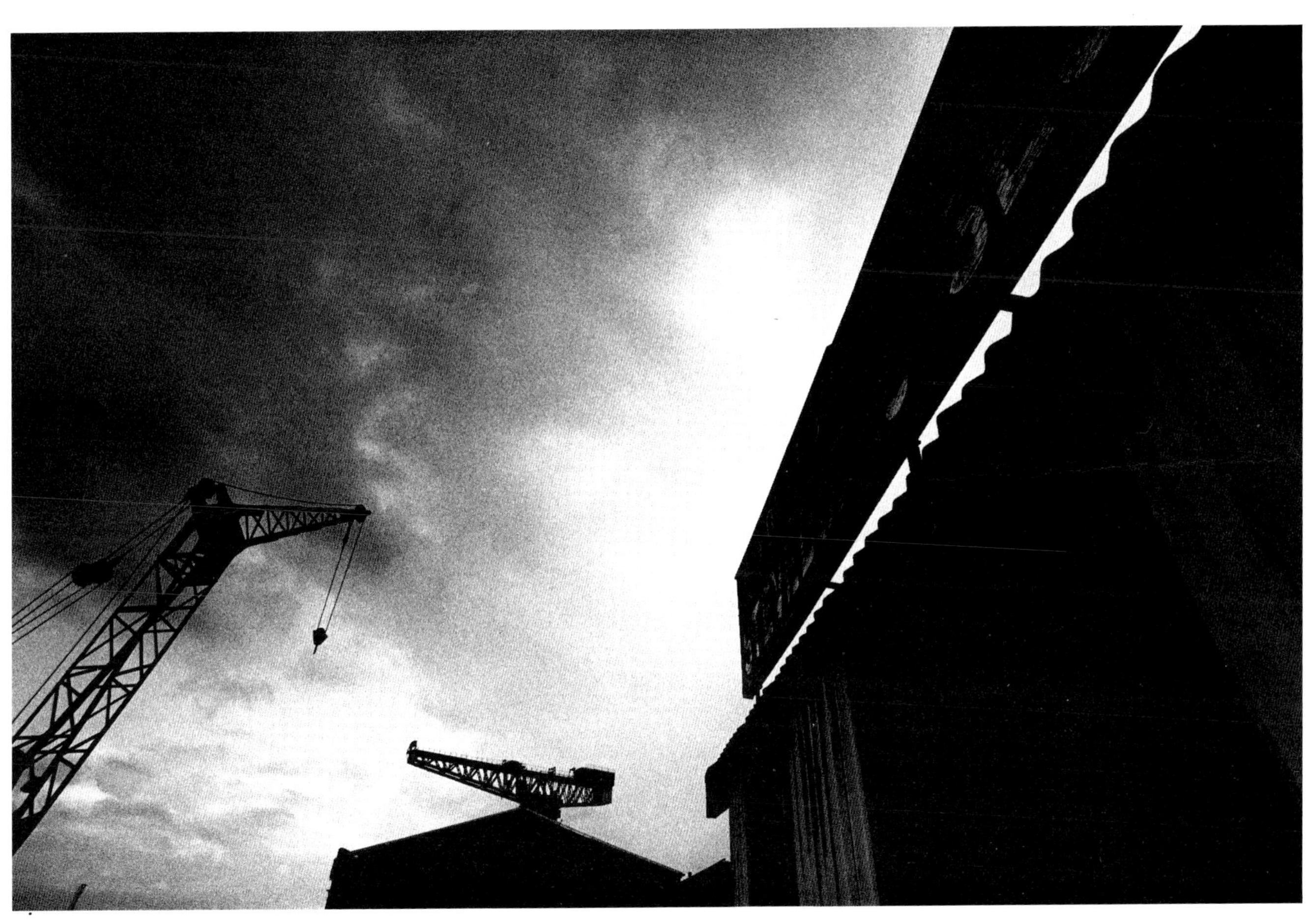

Stevedore secretary's hut
Dockyard, Port Glasgow

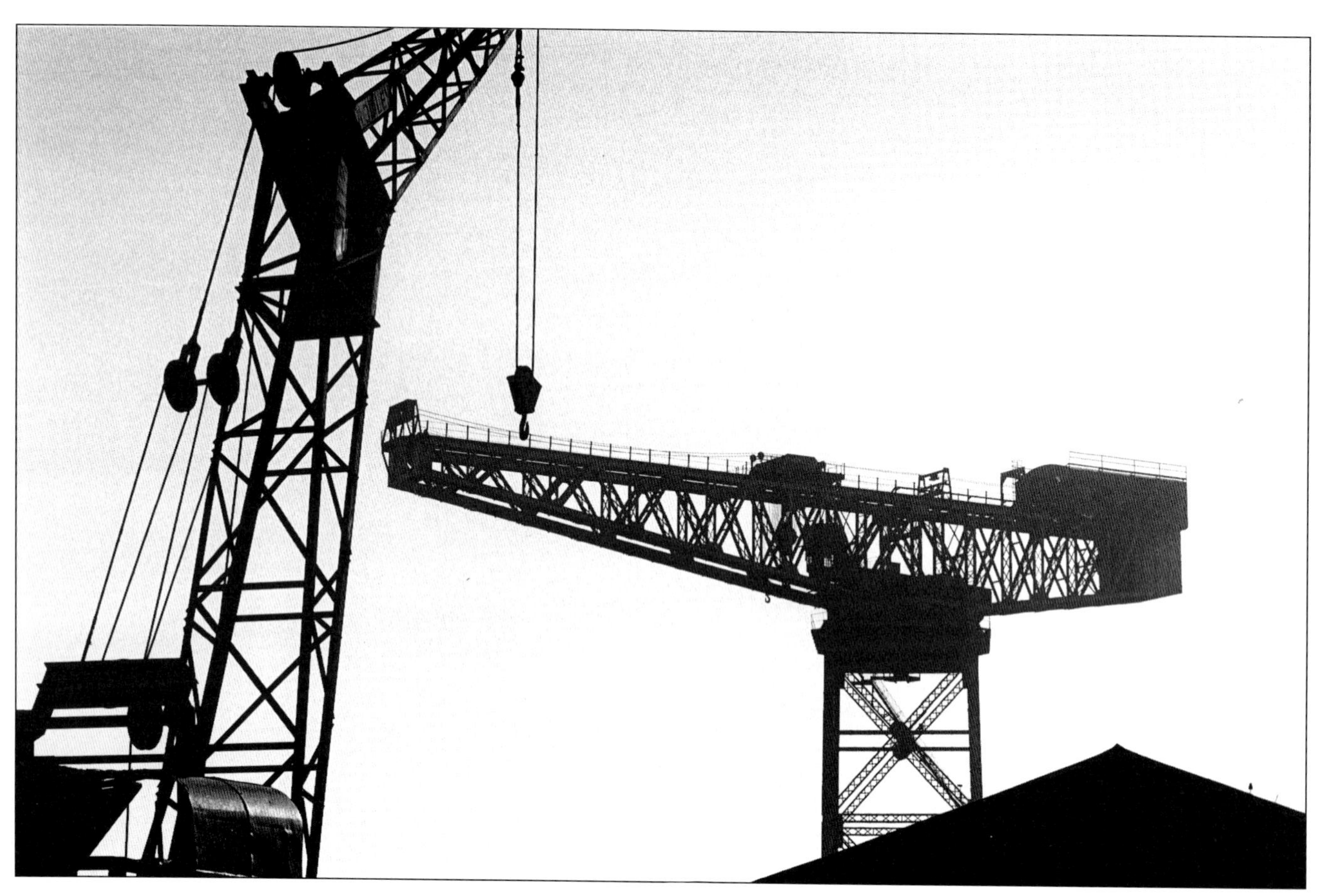

Obsolete shipyards, Glasgow

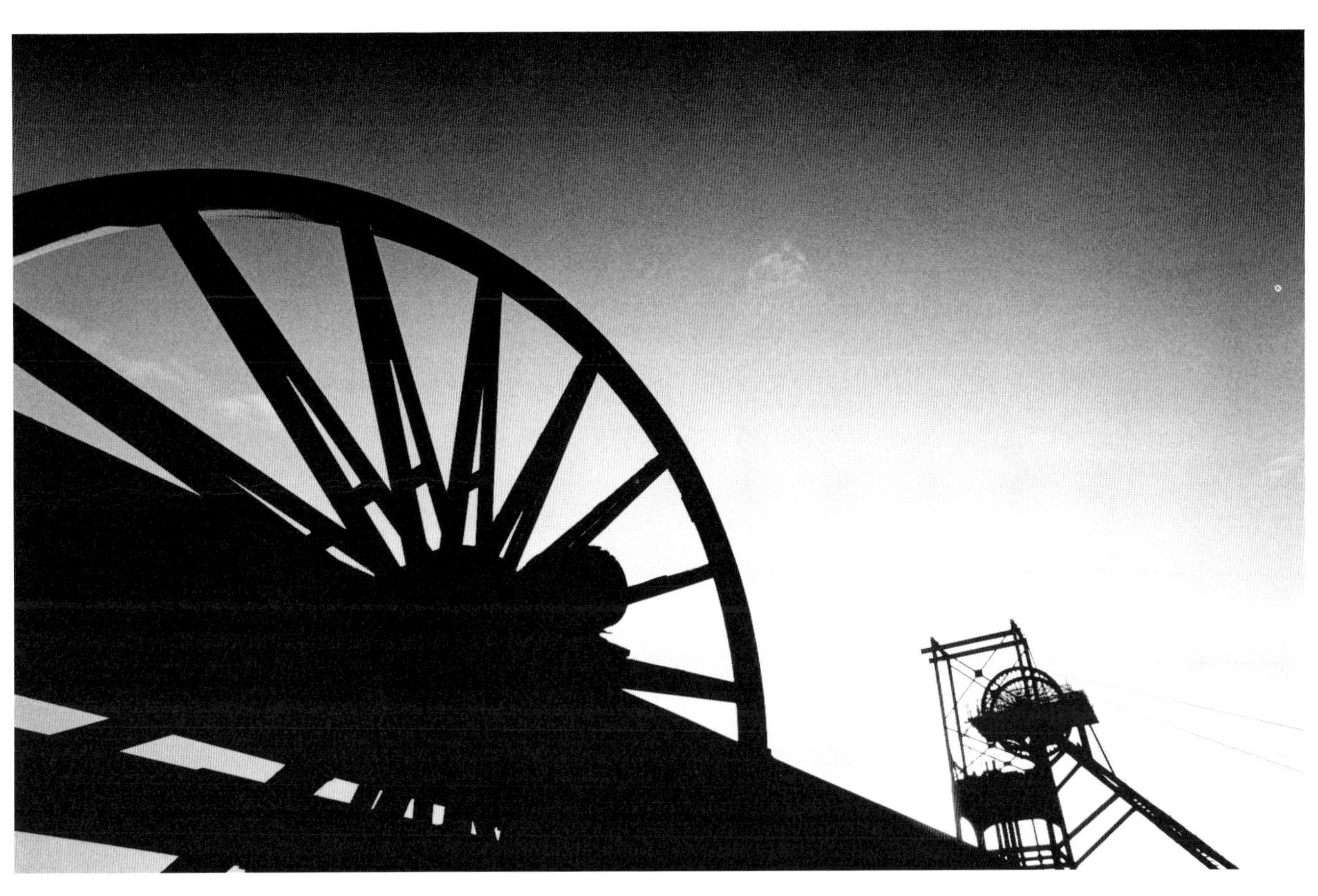

Pithead winding gear
Penalta, South Wales

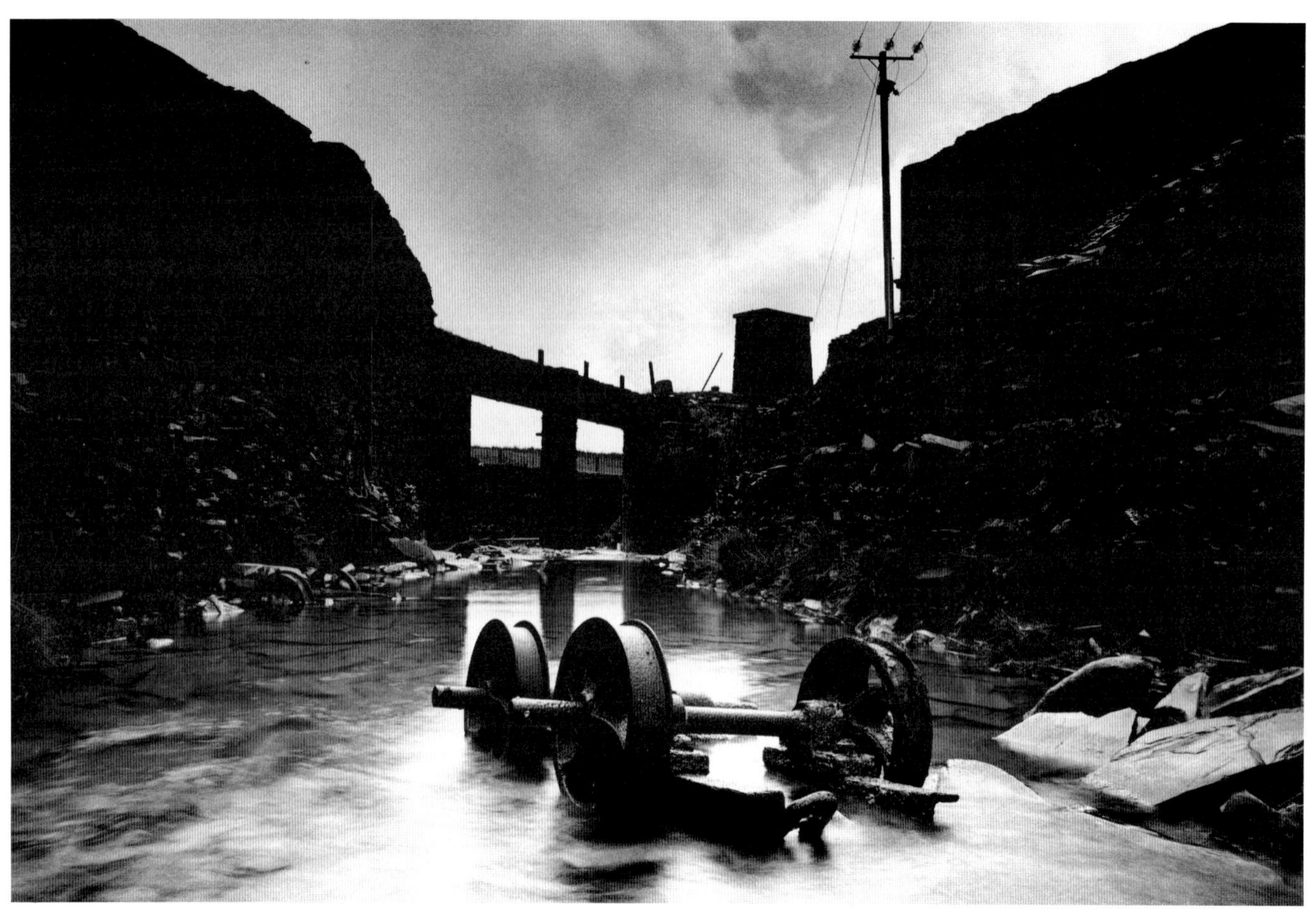

Slate relics
North Wales

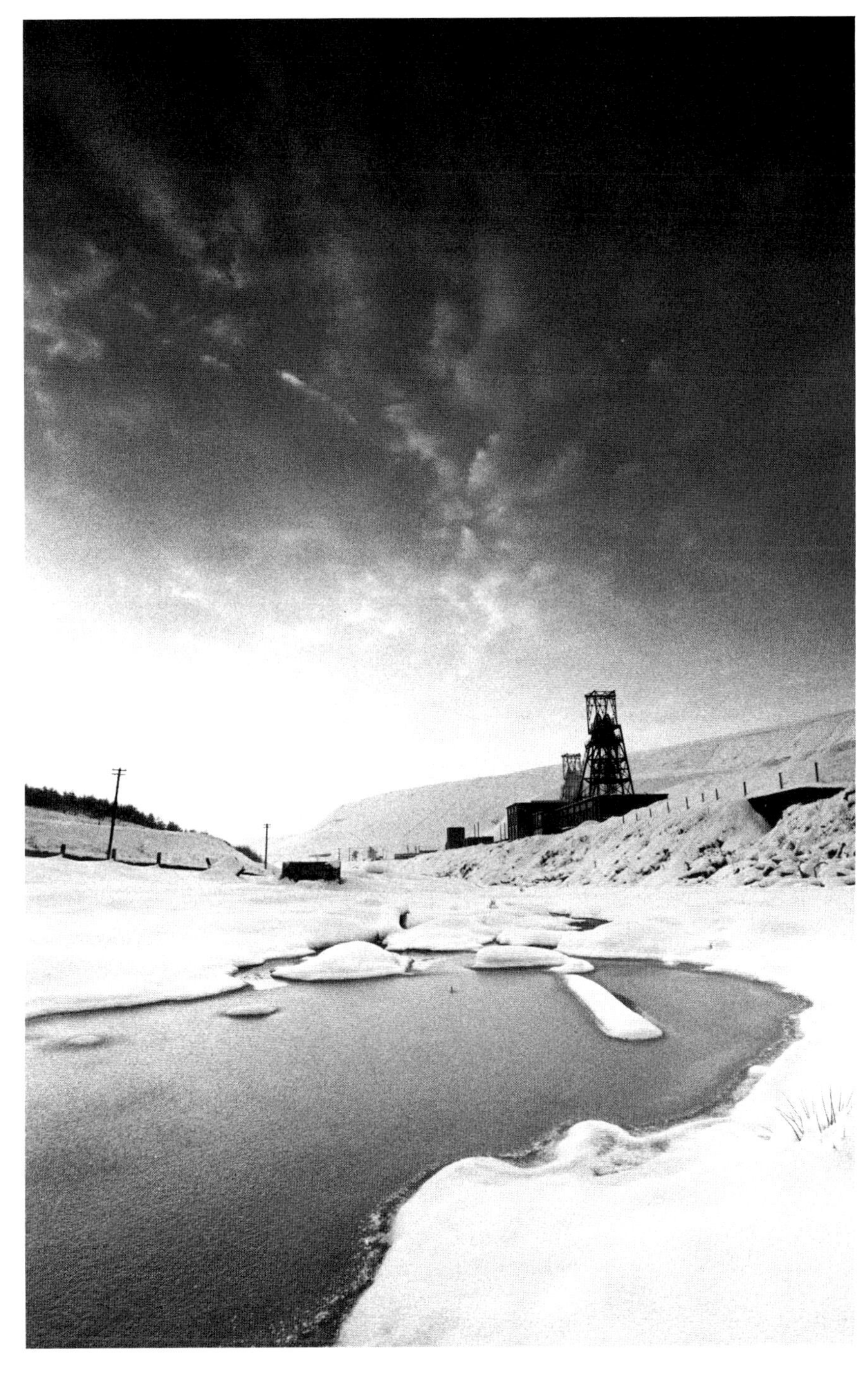

Maerdy colliery
Little Rhondda Valley, Wales

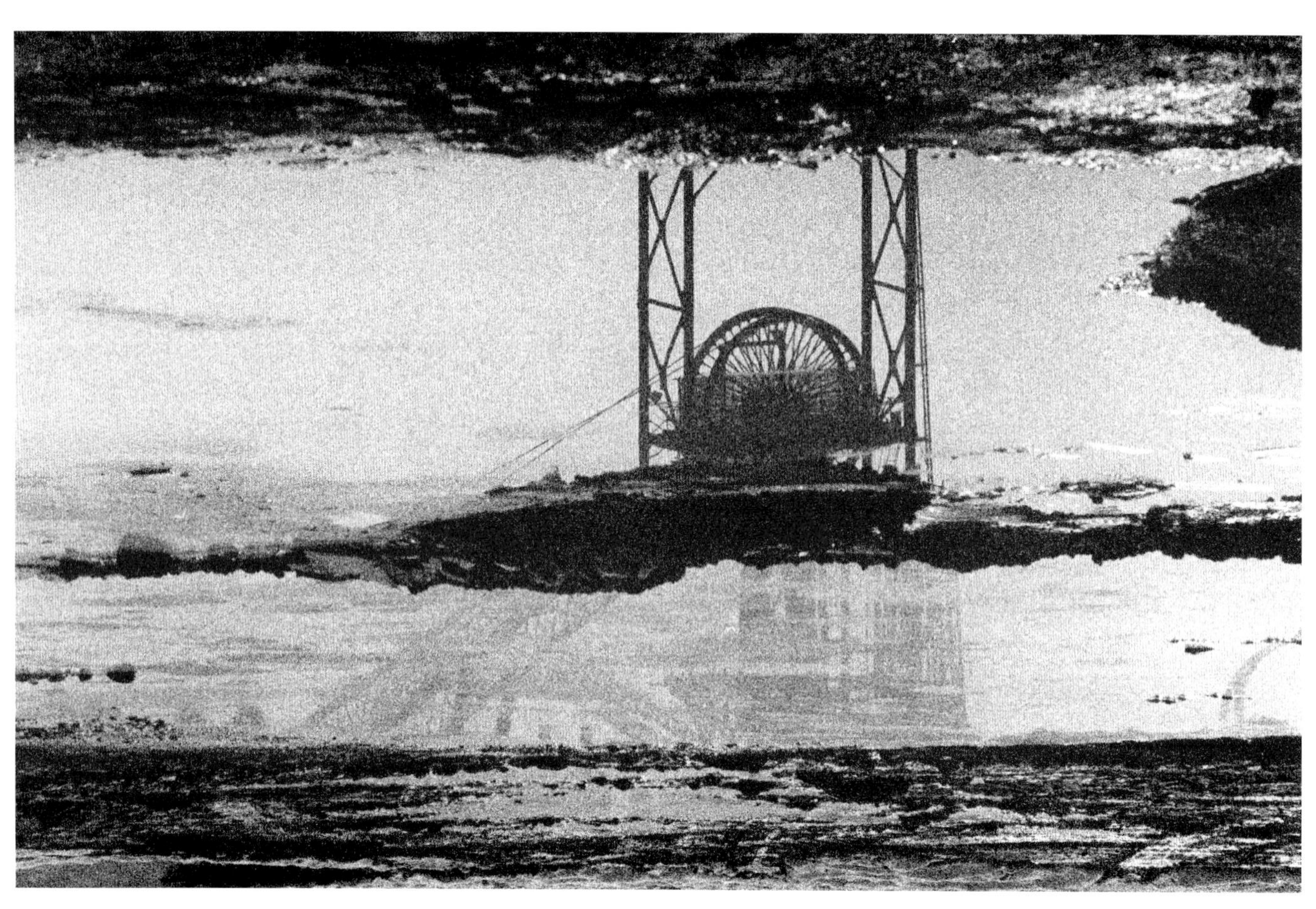

Mine reflection
Treharris, South Wales

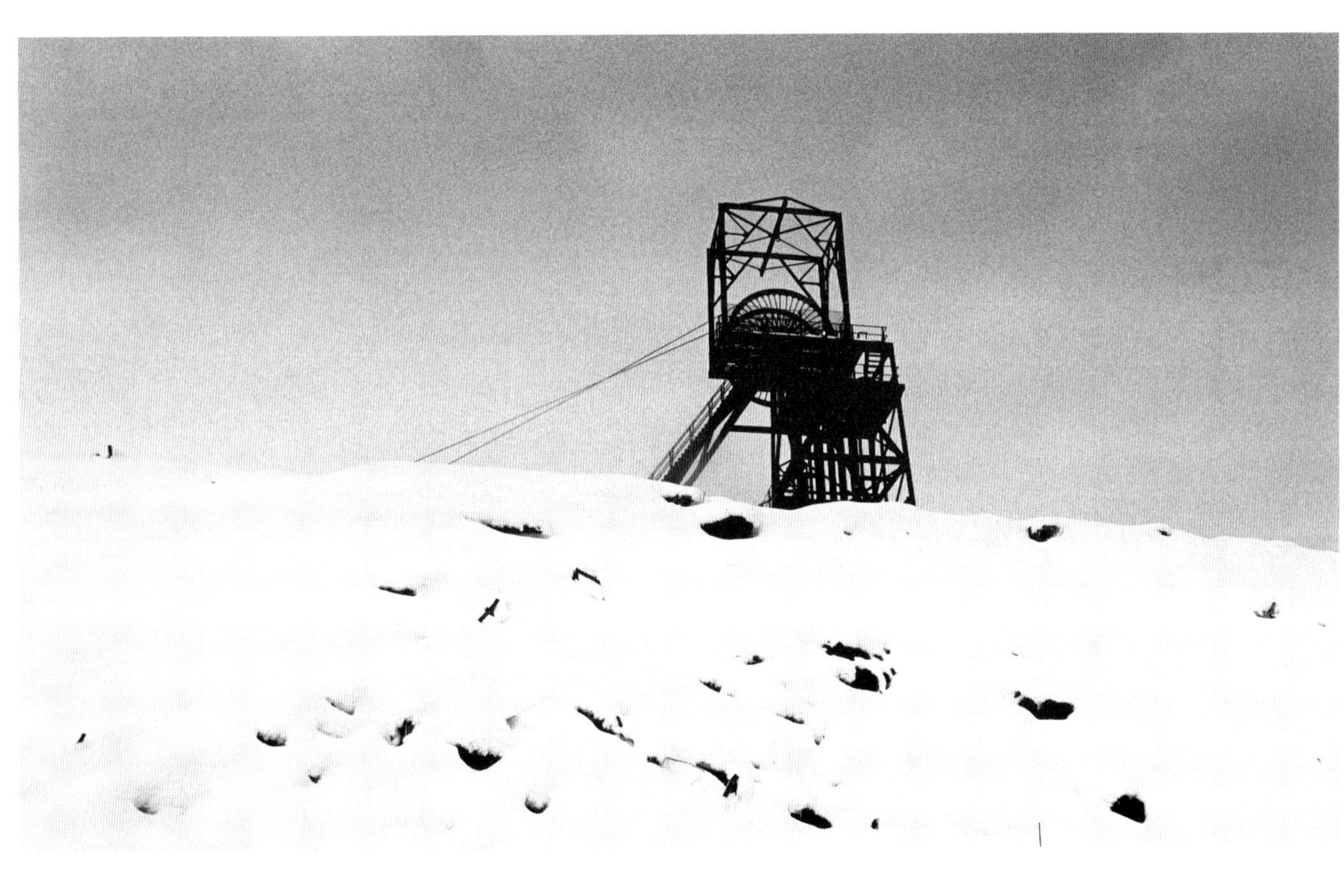

Pit head and snow
South Wales

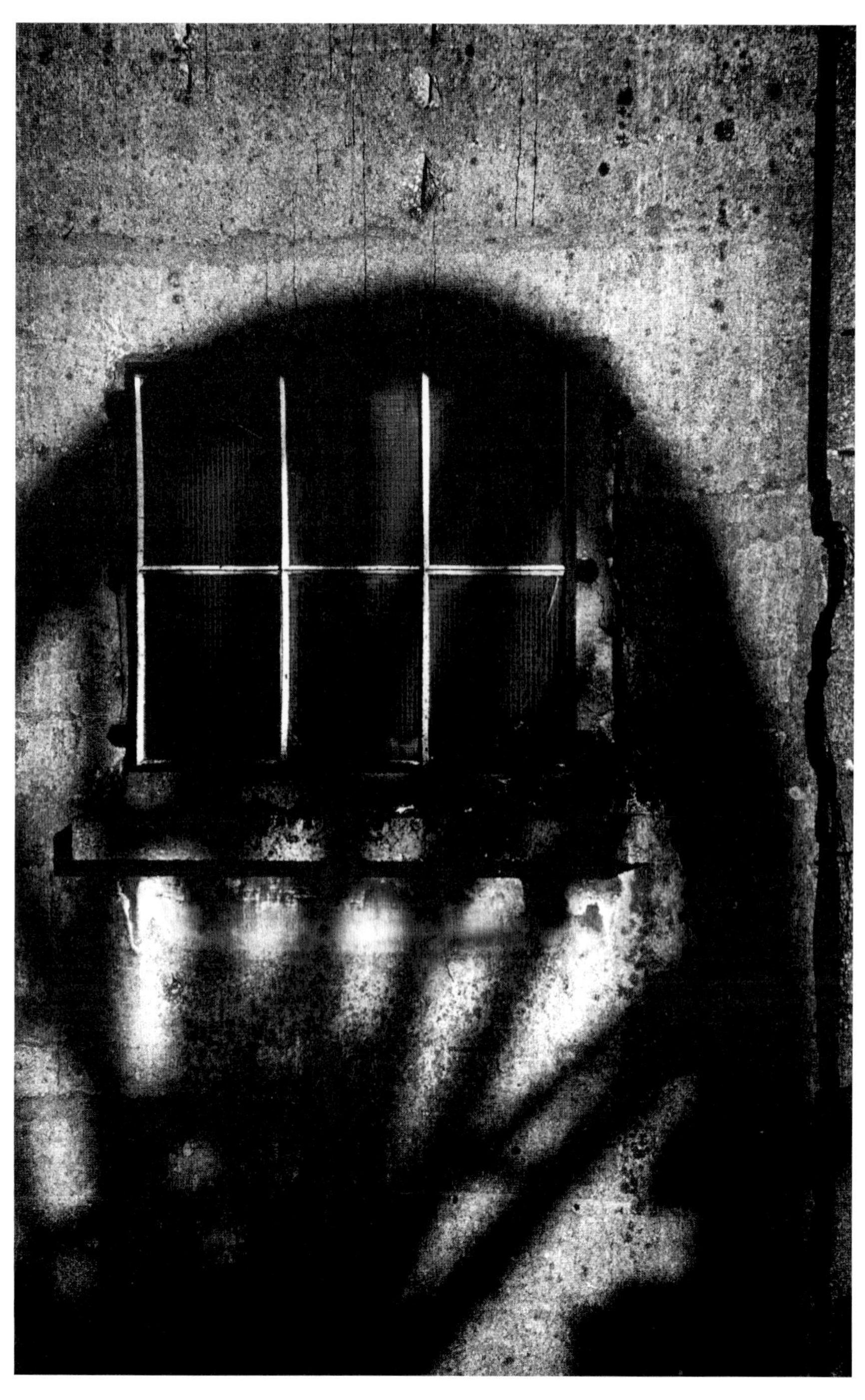

Mine wheel shadow
Rhymney Valley

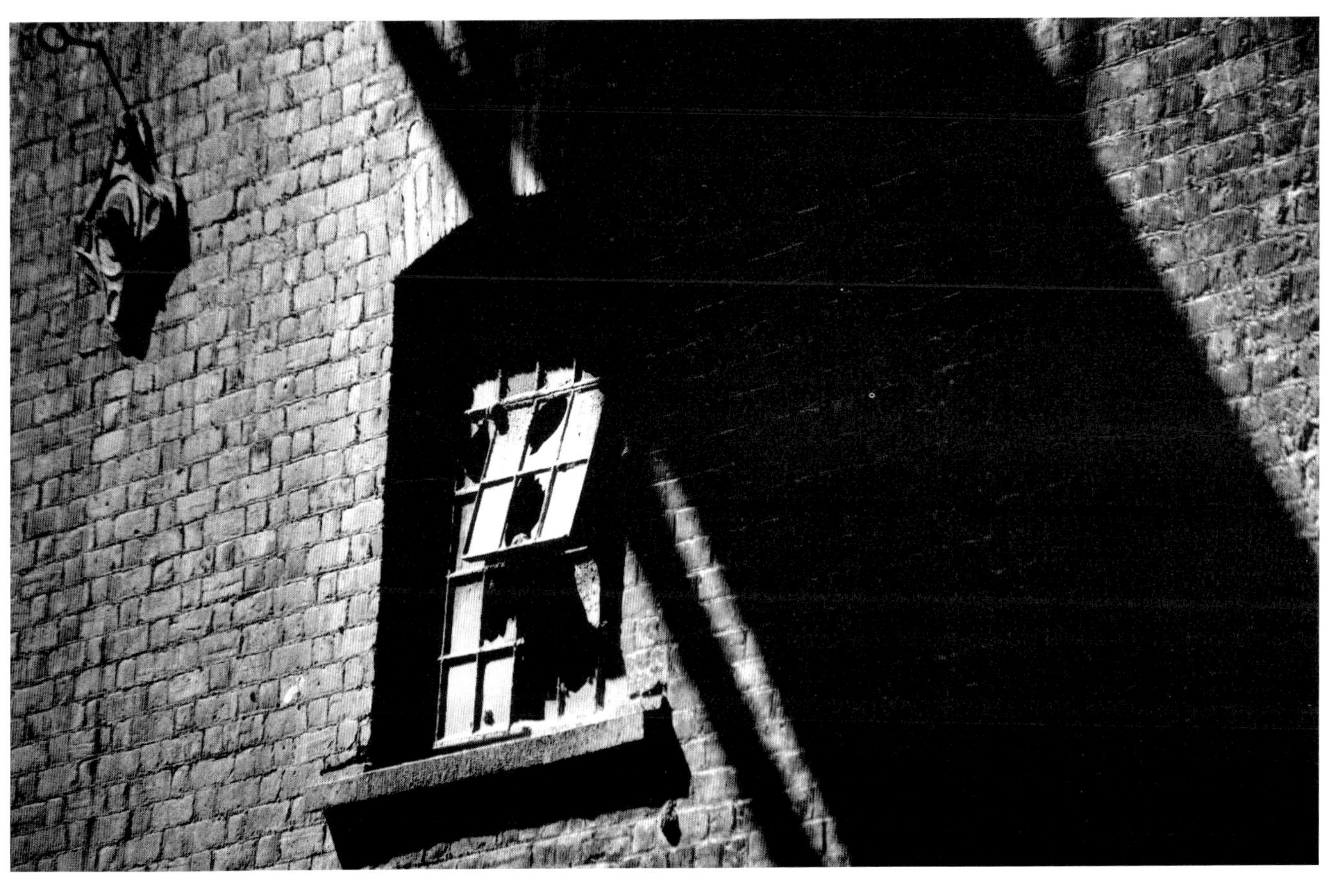

Wharf wall and shadow
Bermondsey, London

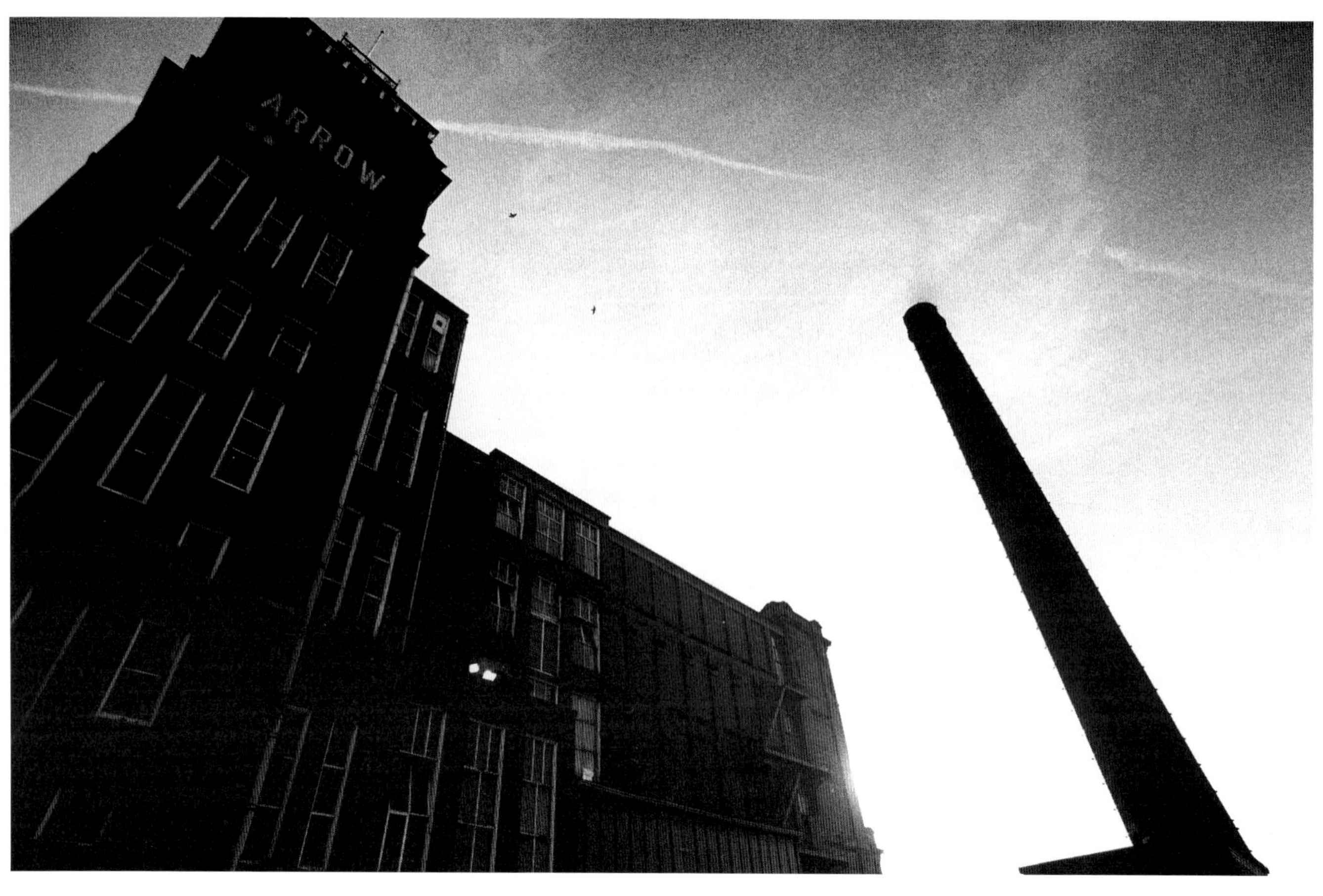

Arrow Mill
Rochdale, Lancashire

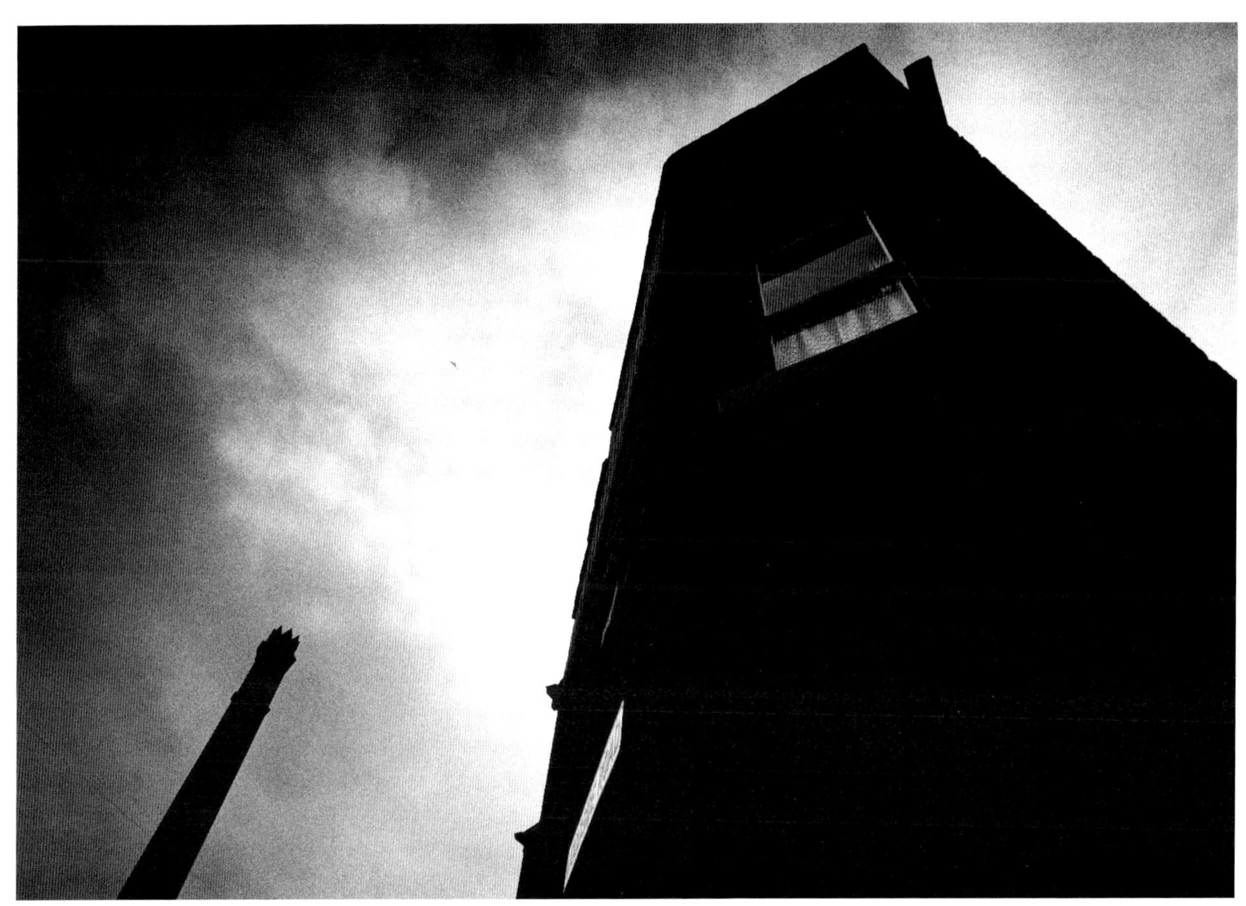

End terrace
Halifax

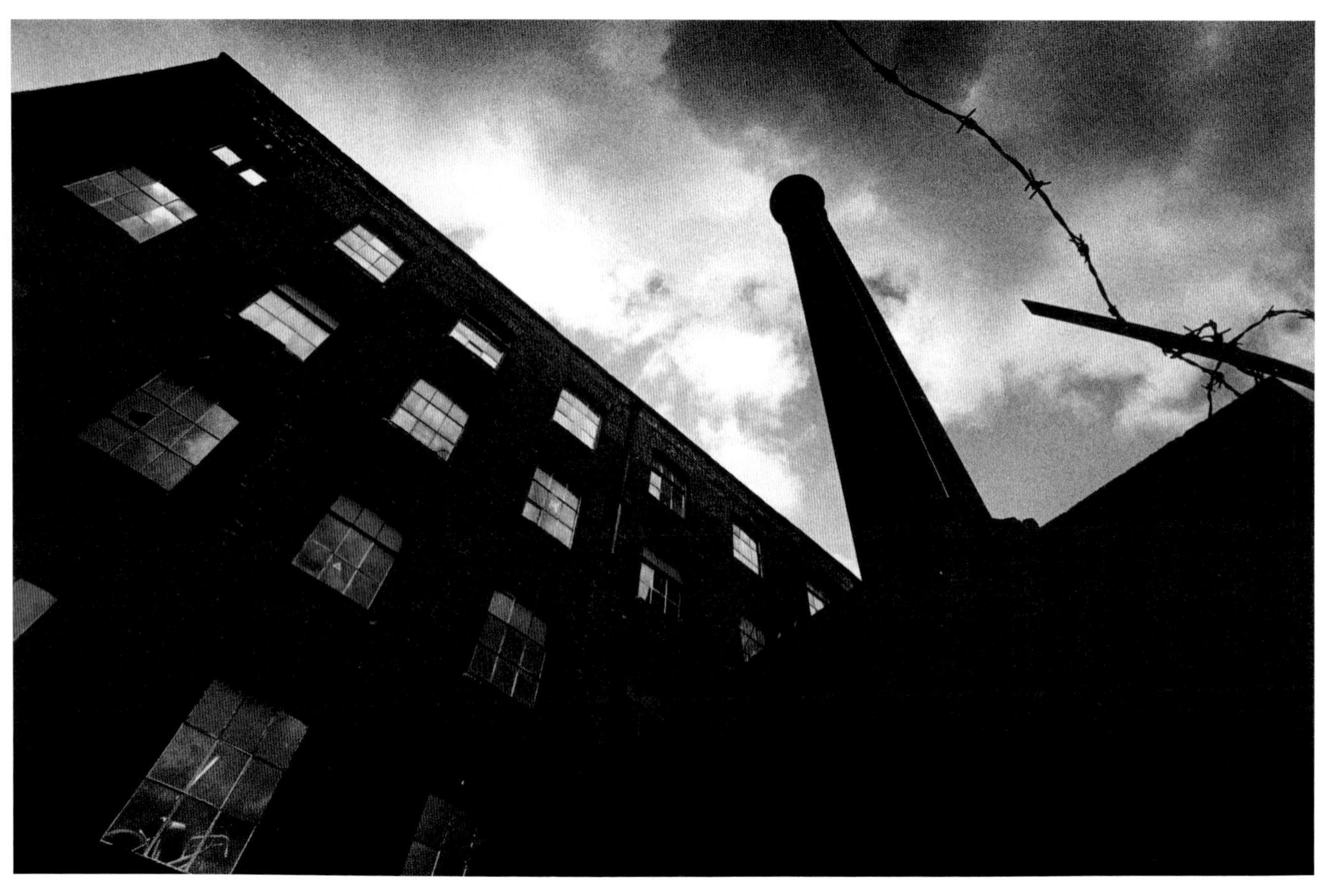

Mill and chimney
Stockport, Greater Manchester

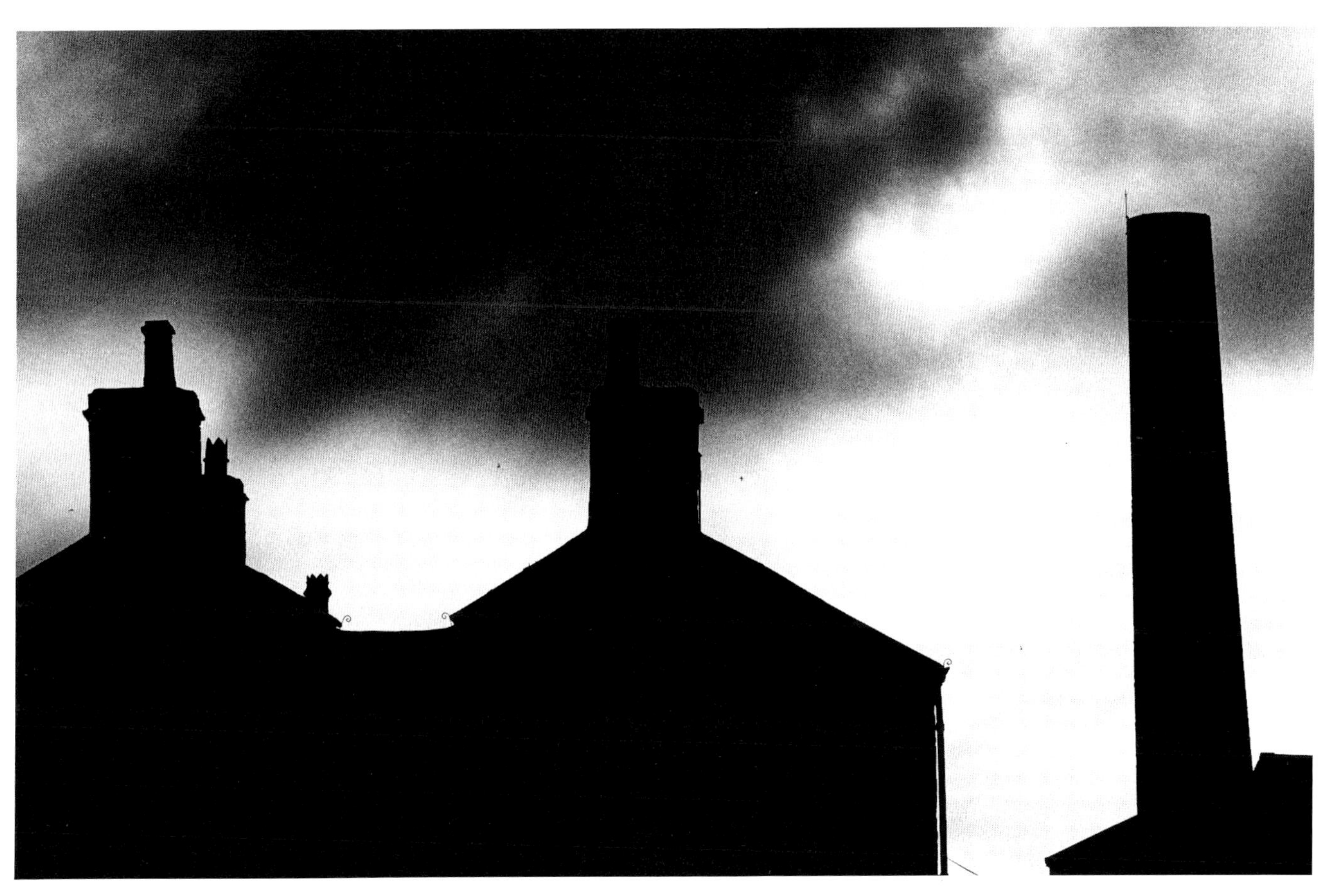

Mill and cottages
Marsden, West Yorkshire

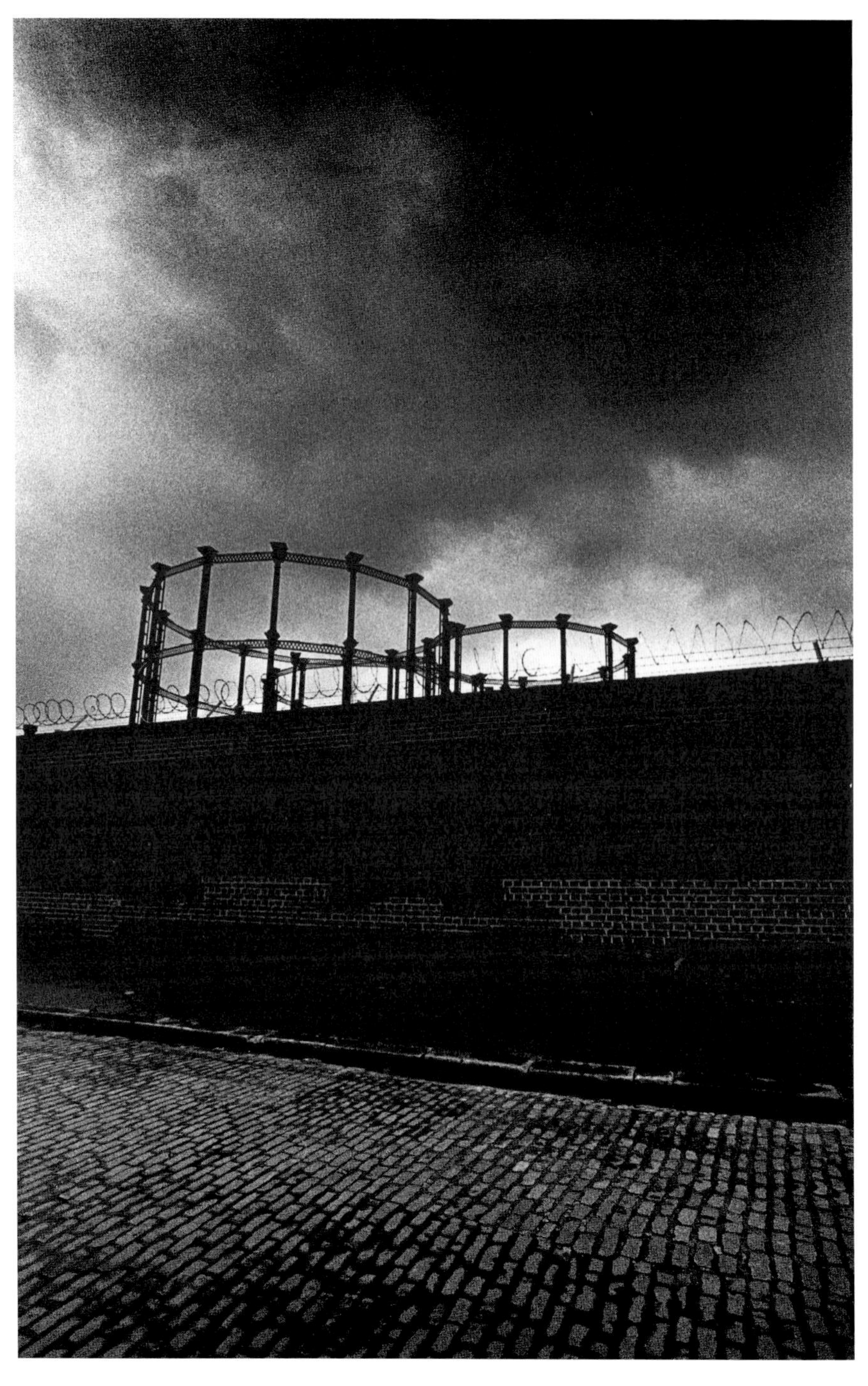

Goods Way
Kings Cross, London

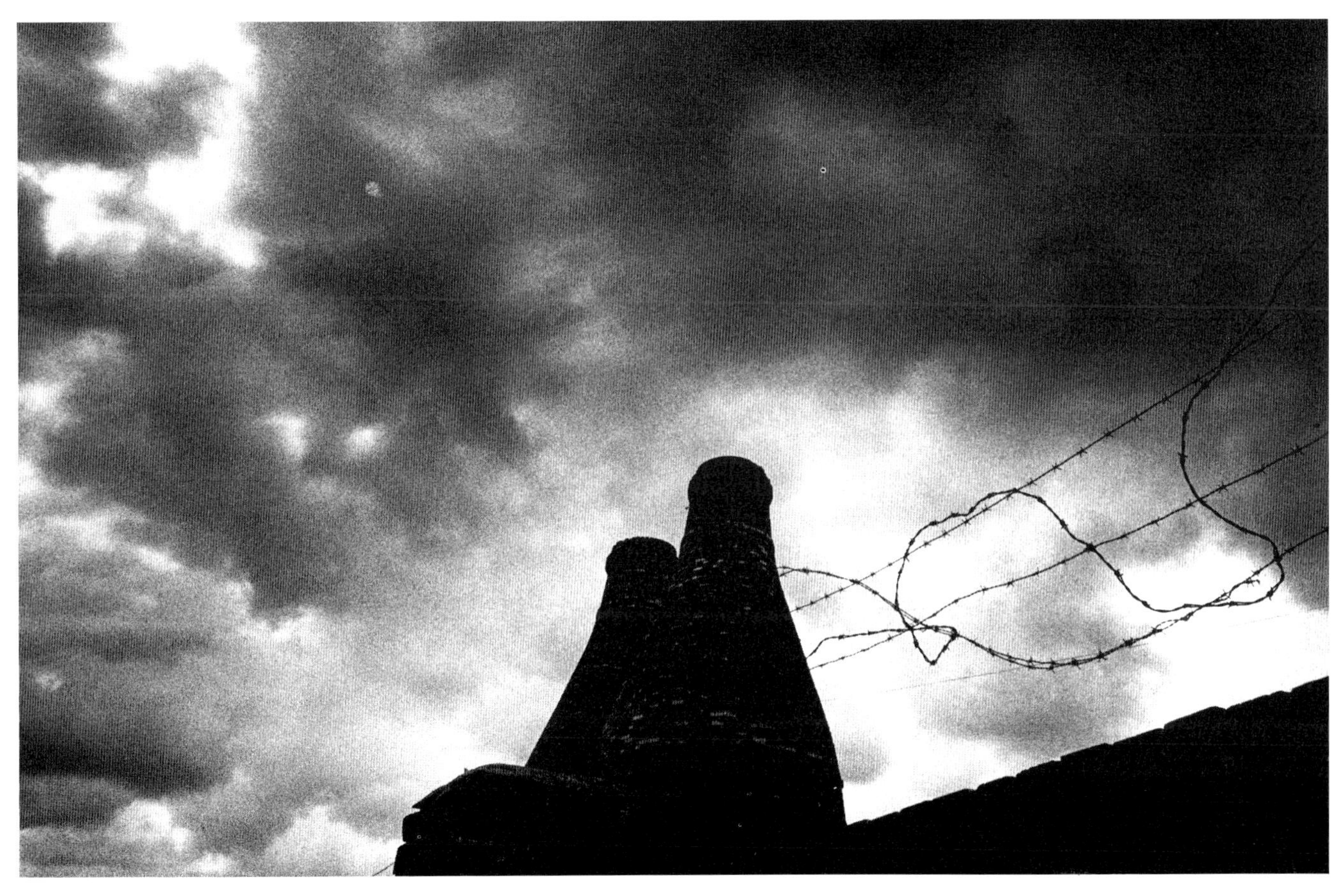

Disused pot banks
Hanley, Stoke-on-Trent

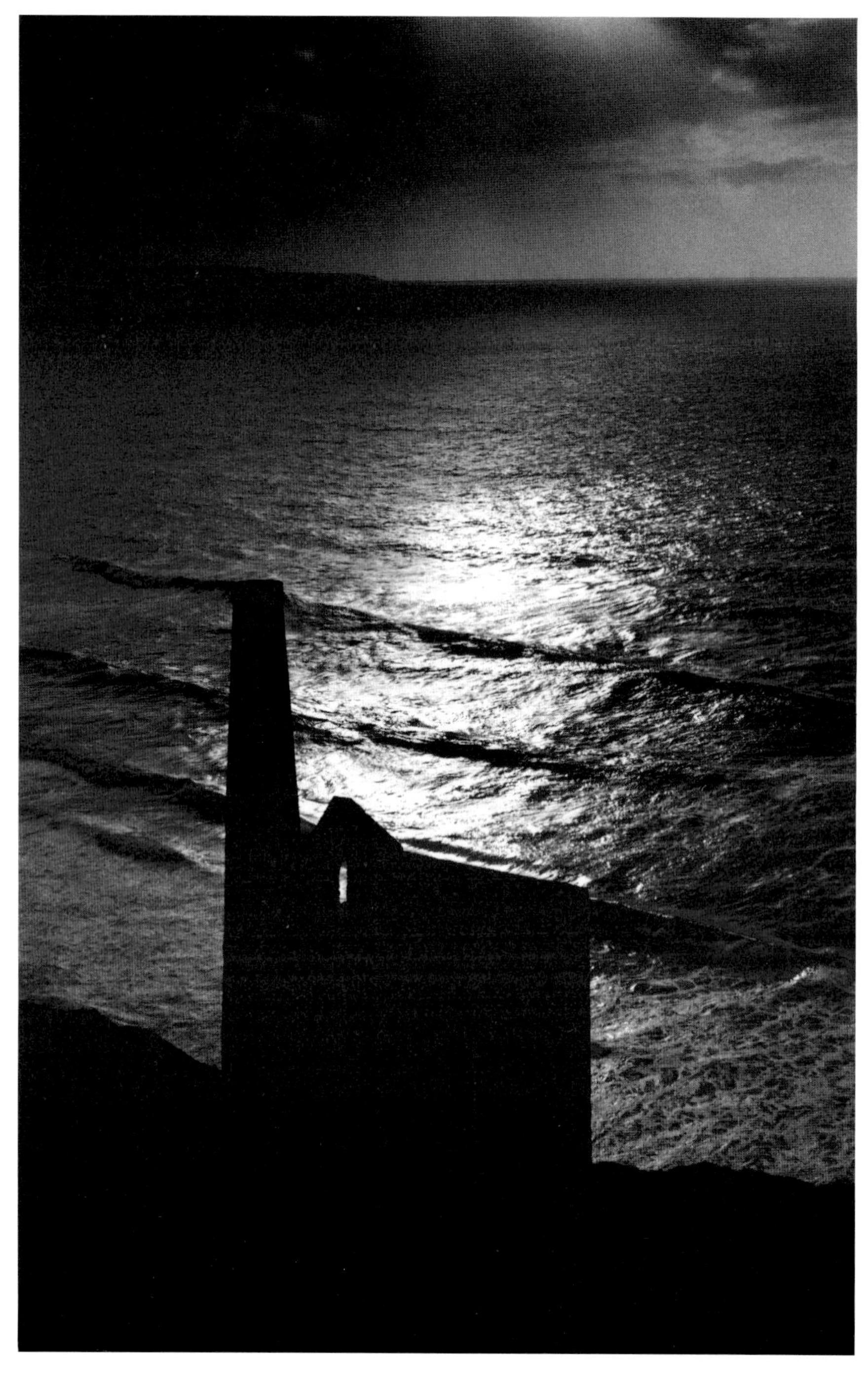

Tin mine engine house
North Cornwall

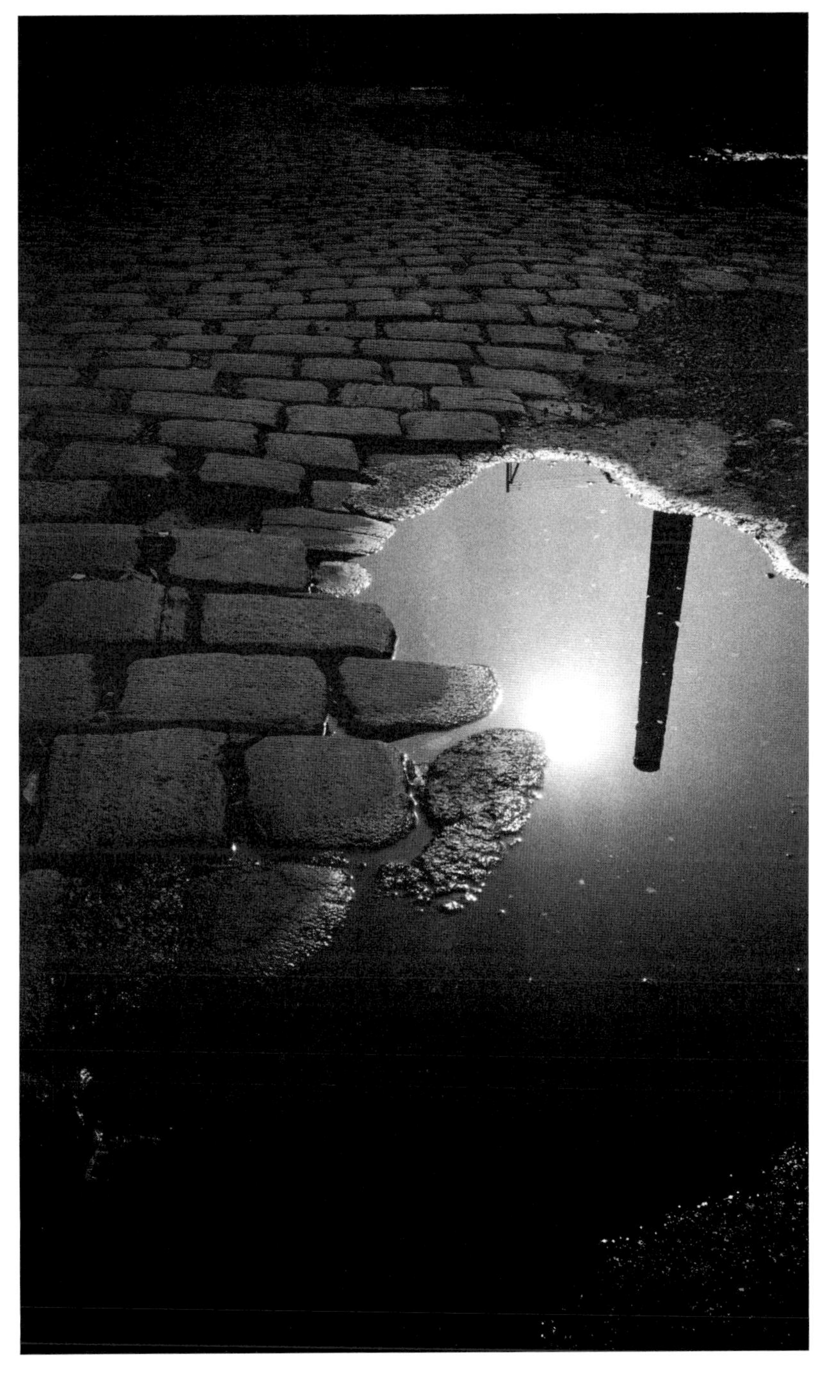

Mill gates and cobbles
Chadderton, Greater Manchester

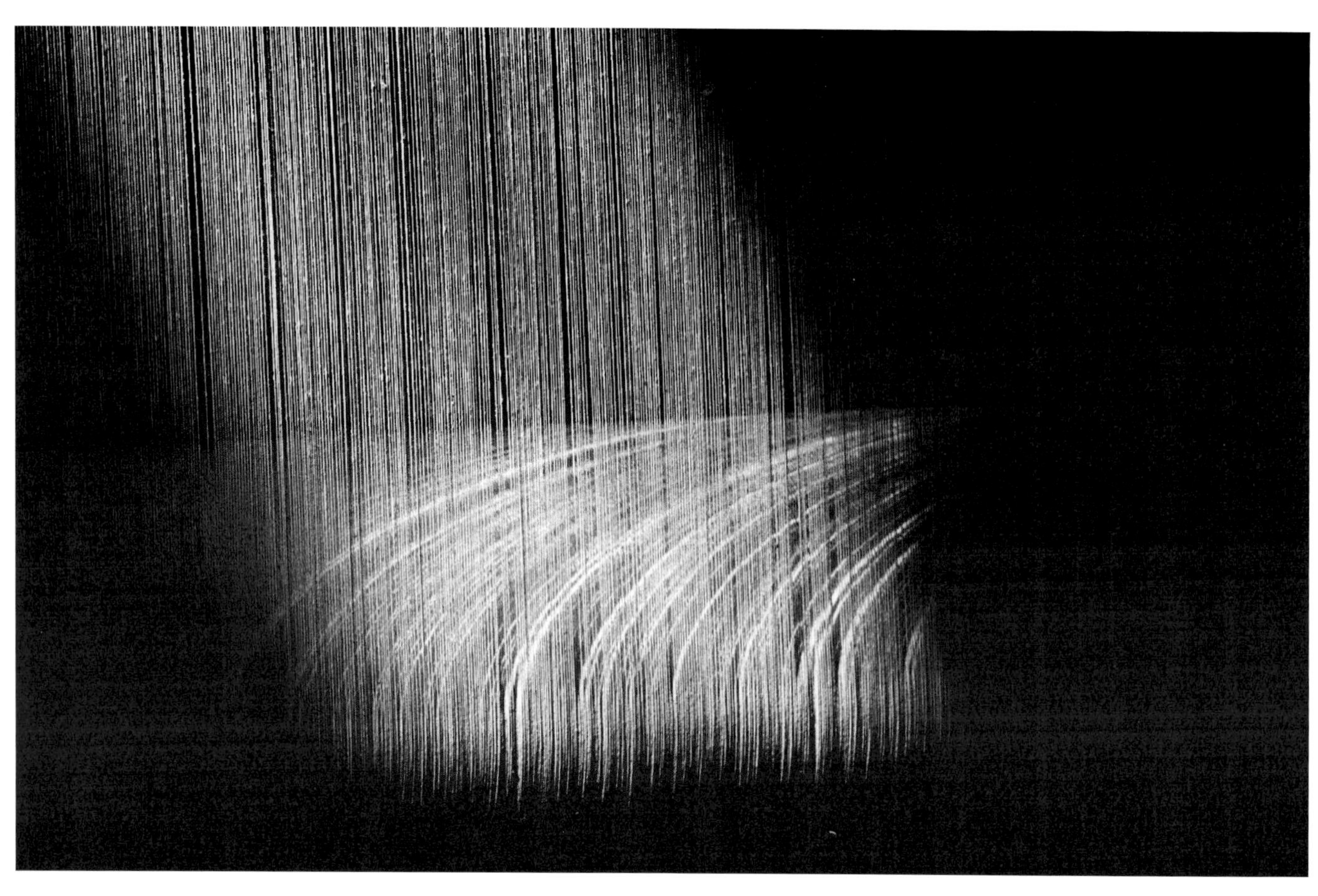

Cotton loom

Harle Syke, Lancashire

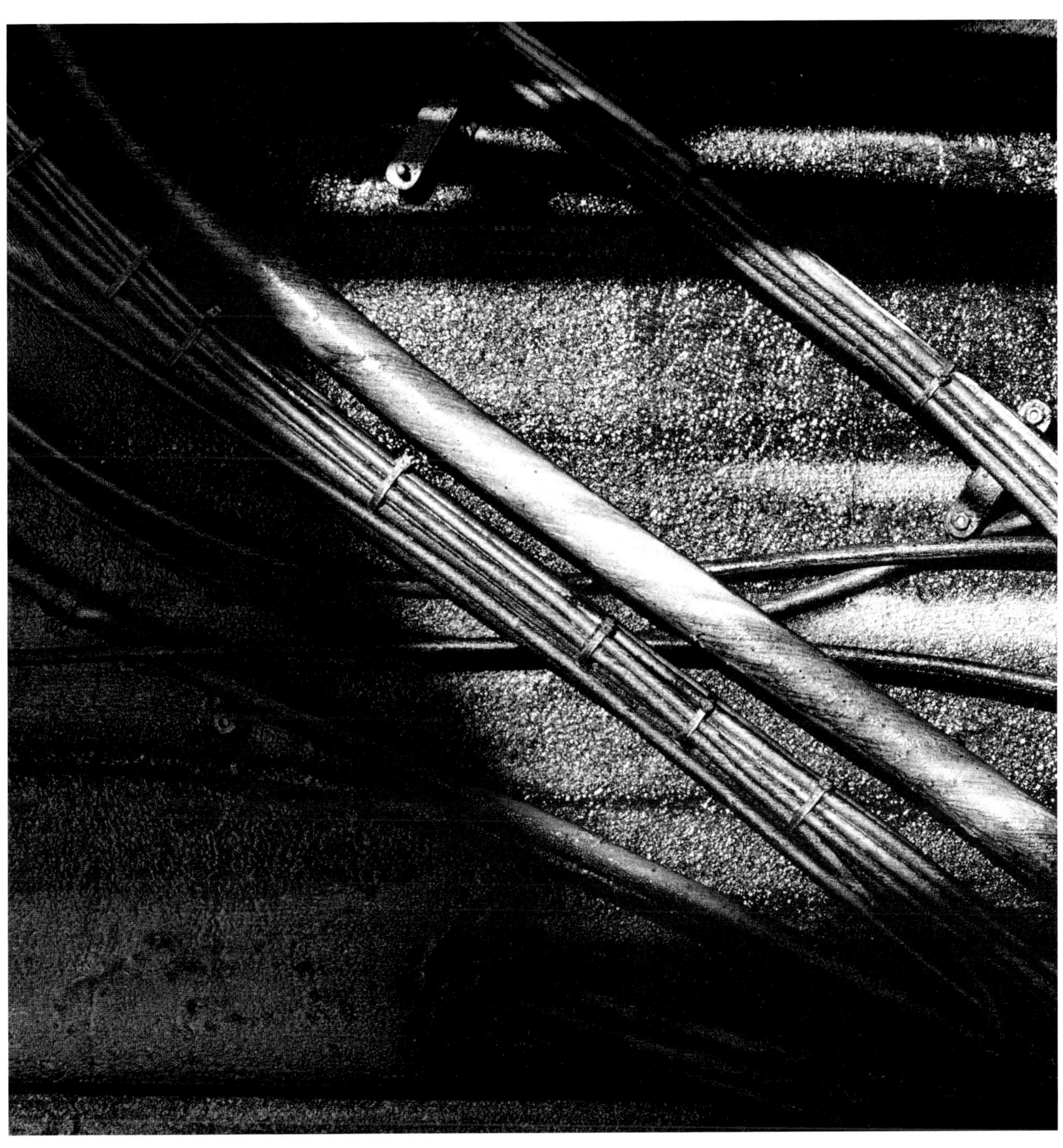

Oil and wires
South Wales

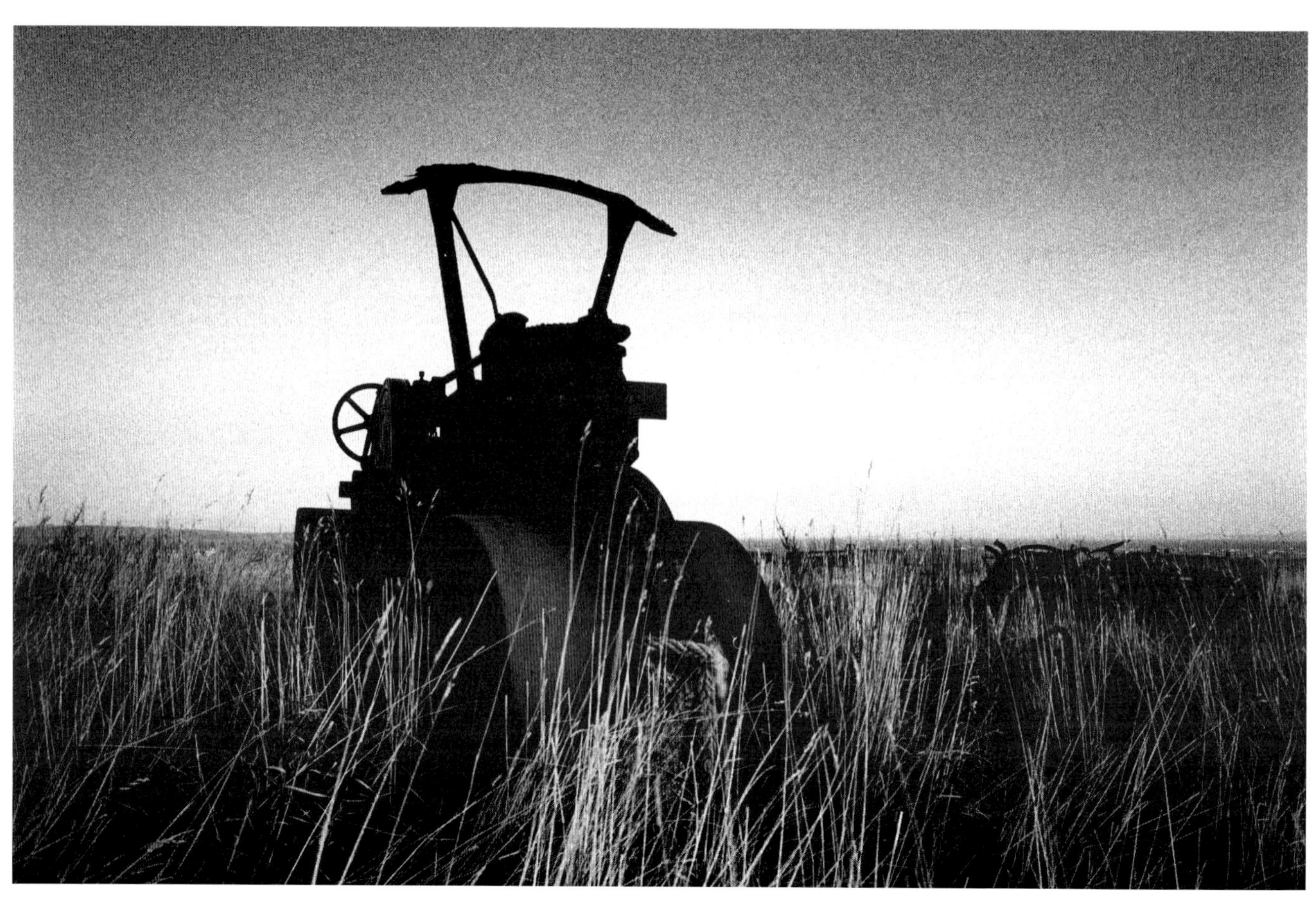

Abandoned traction engine
John o'Groat's

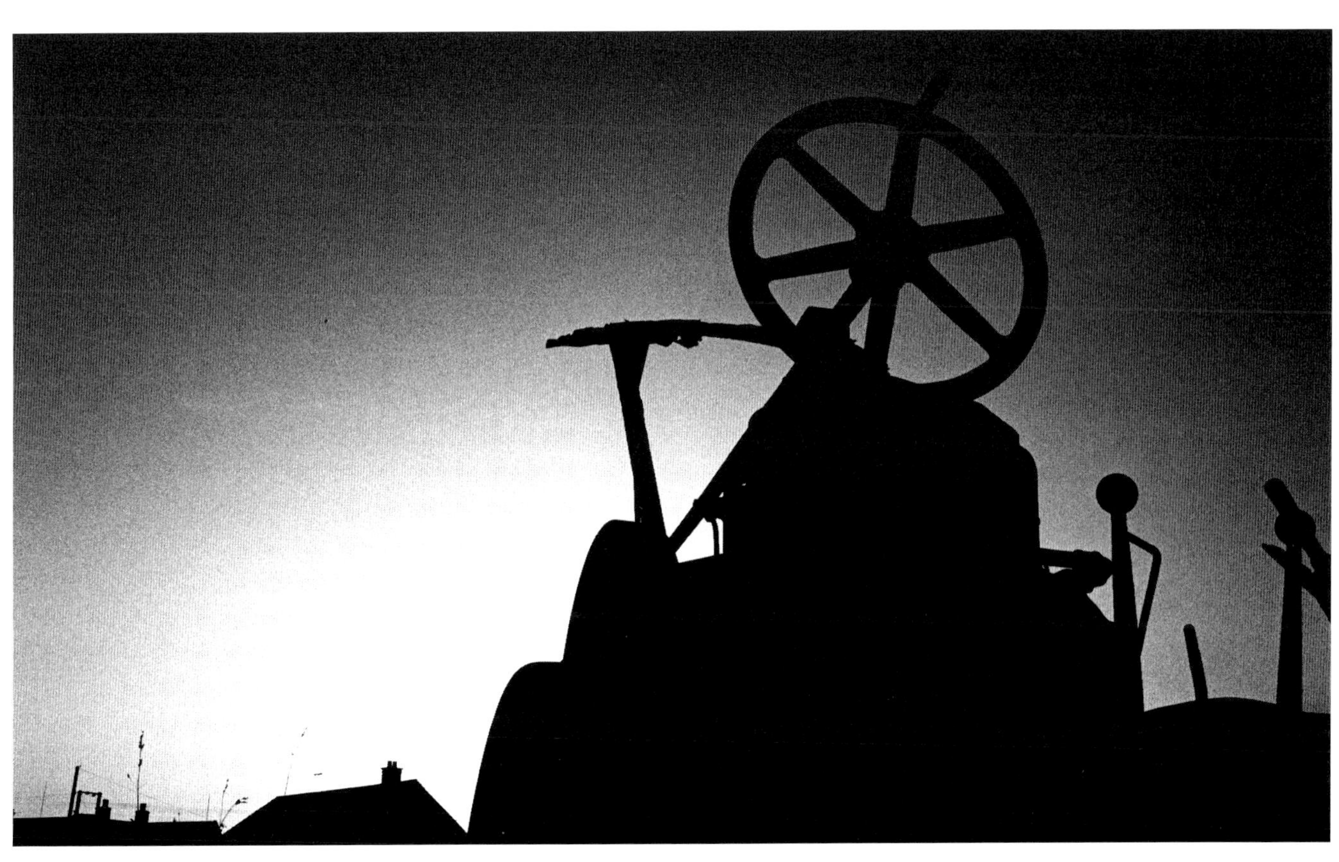

Silhouetted traction engine
Caithness, Scotland

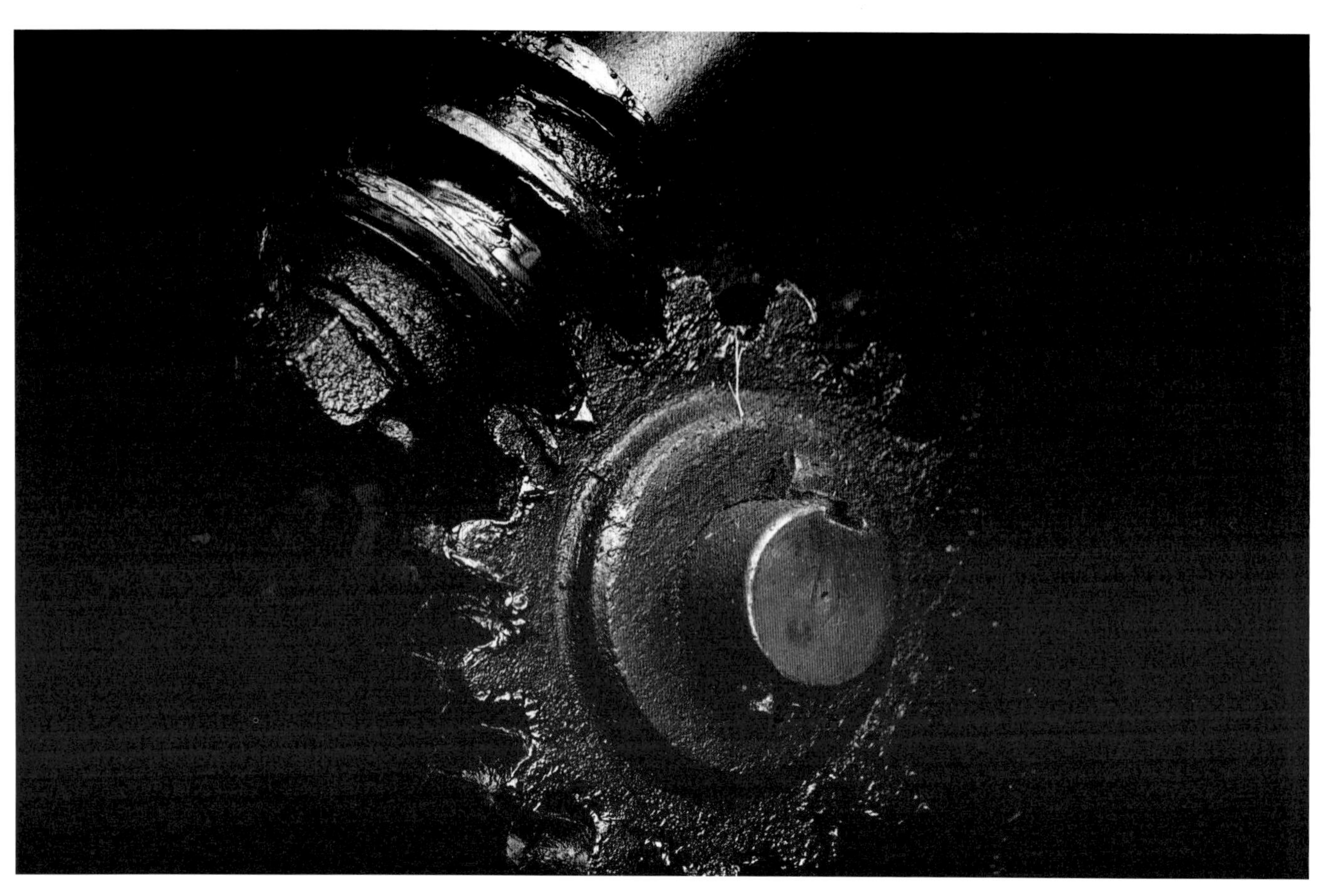

Worm gear and grease

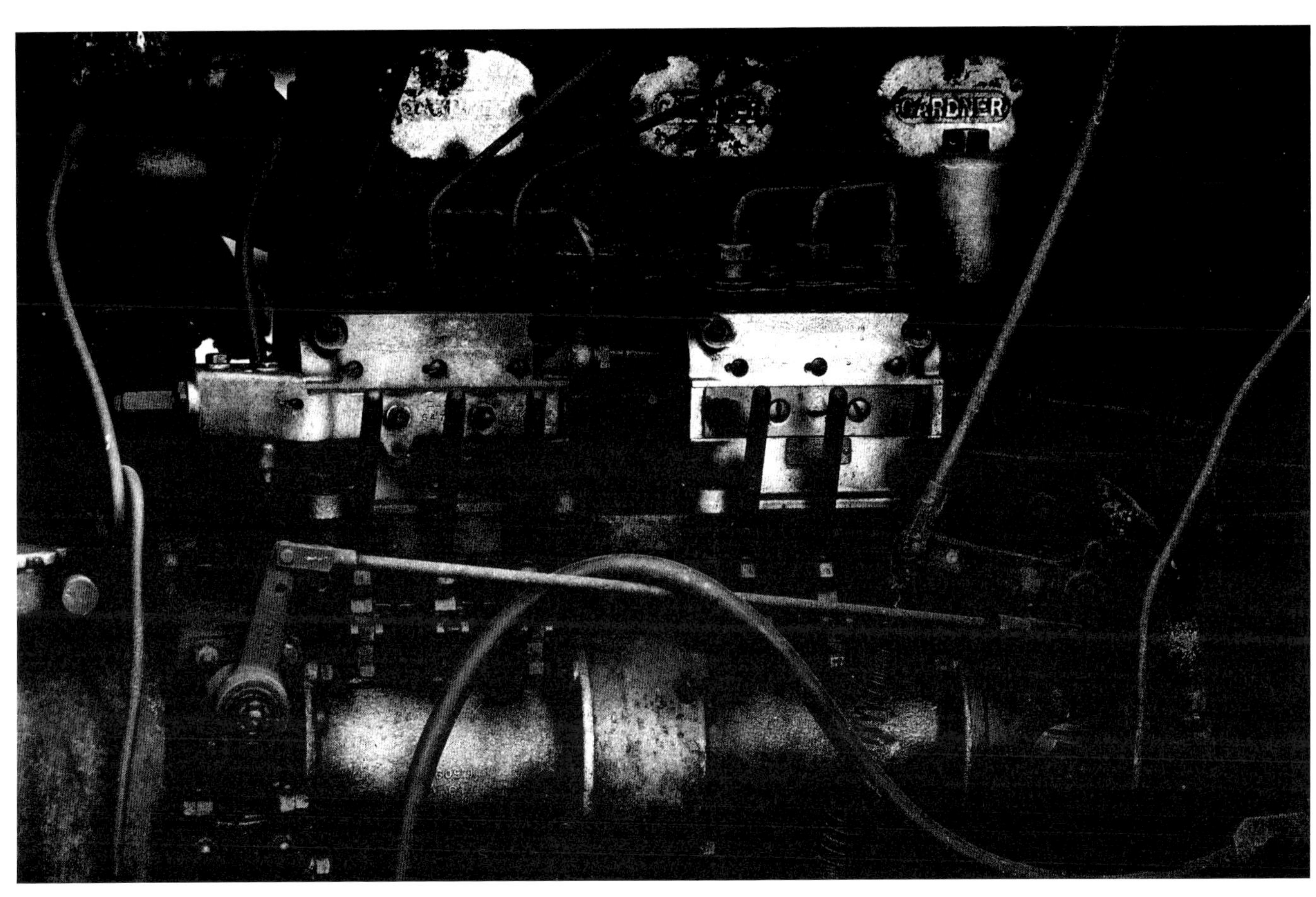

Lorry engine
Knowl Hill, Berkshire

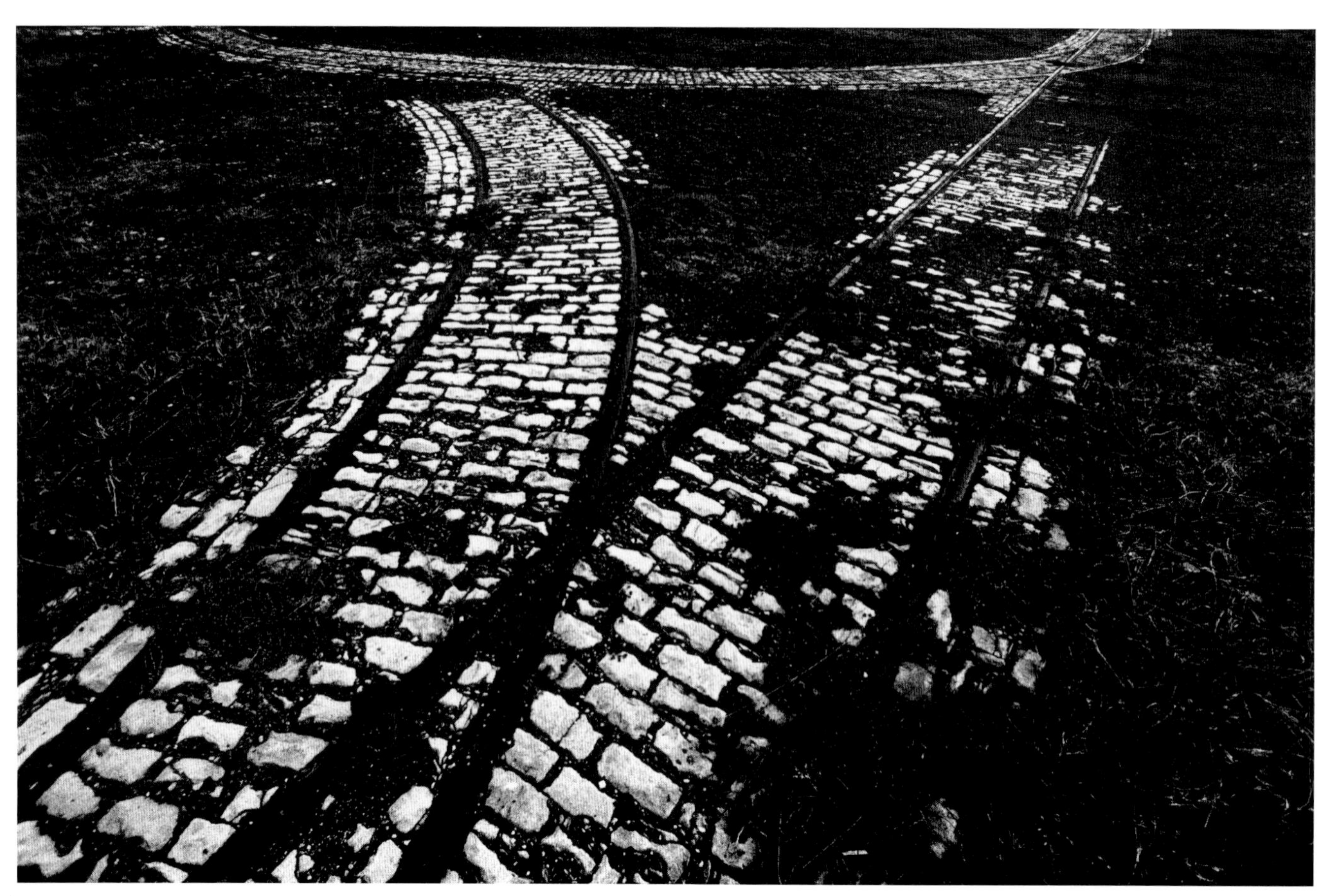

Quayside
Lancaster

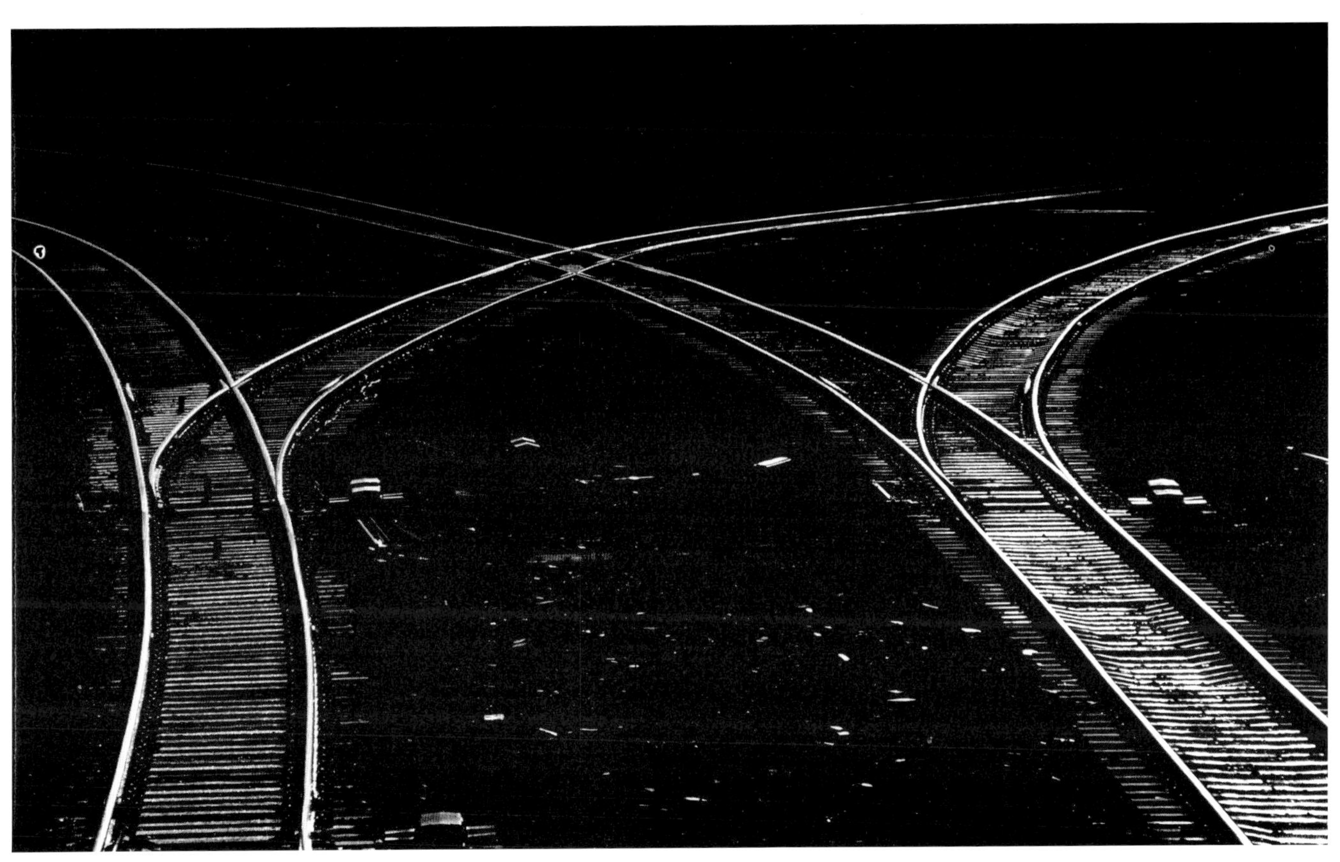

Railway junction
Tyseley, Birmingham

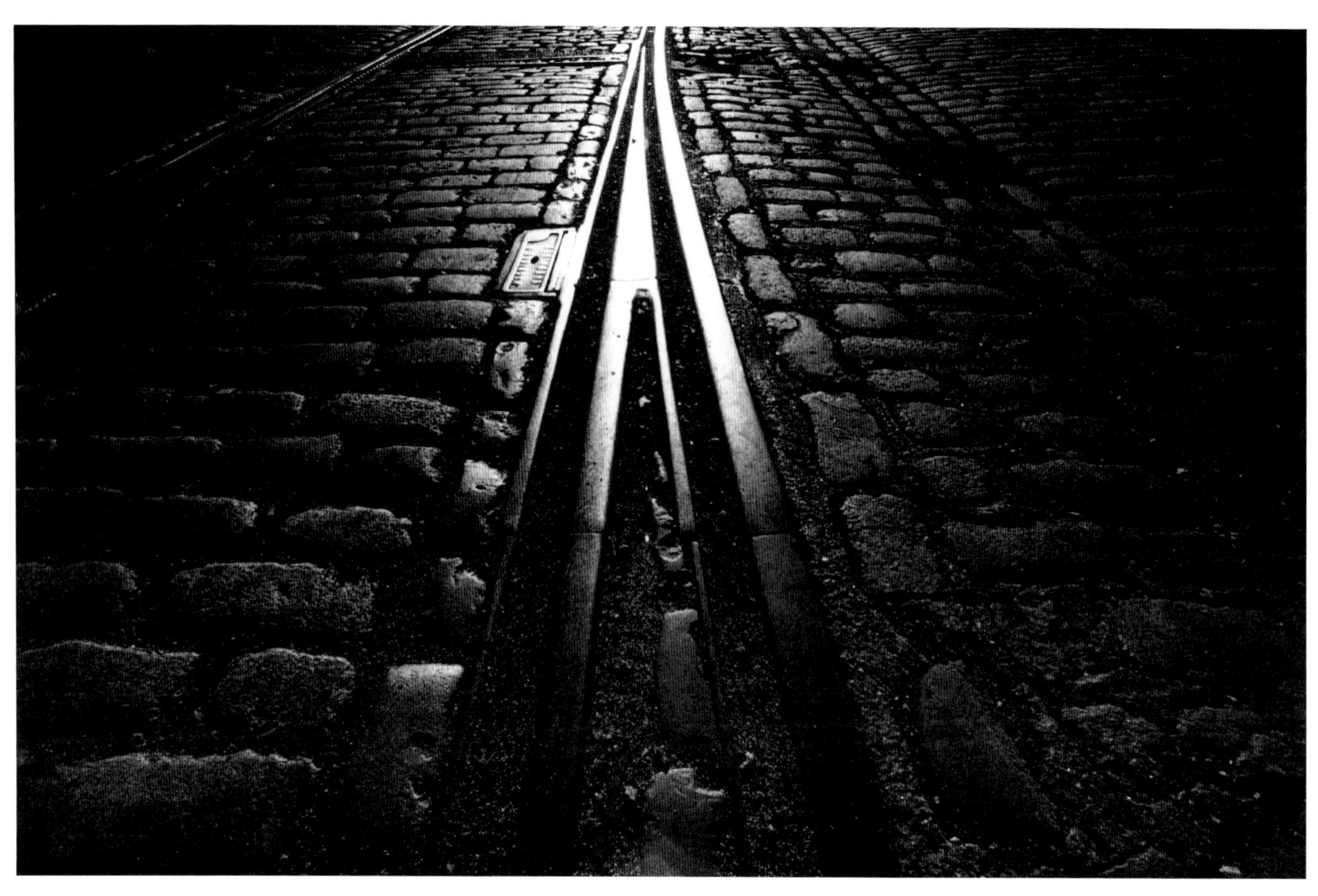

Sunlight and rails
Huskisson dock, Liverpool

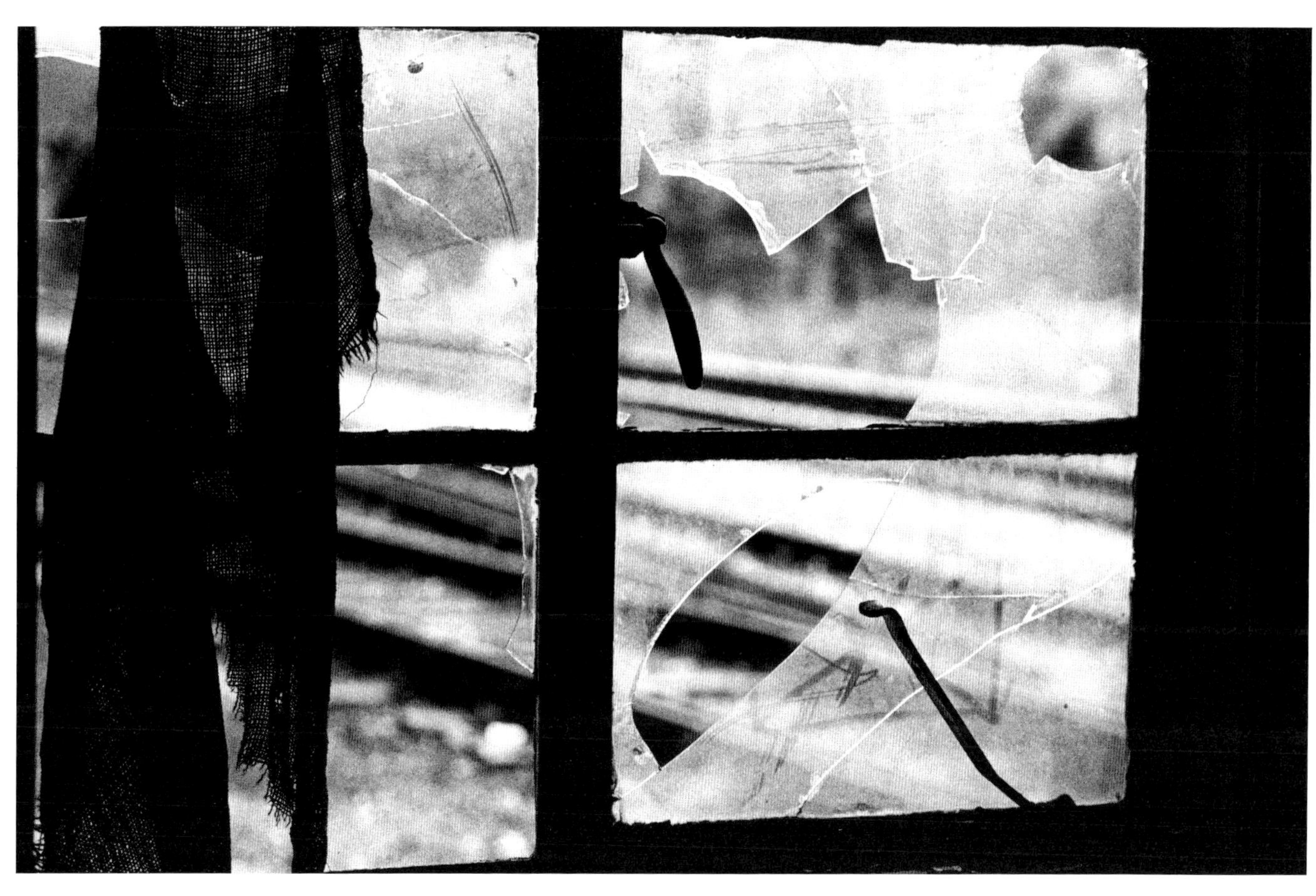

Workman's hut
Stroud station, Gloucestershire

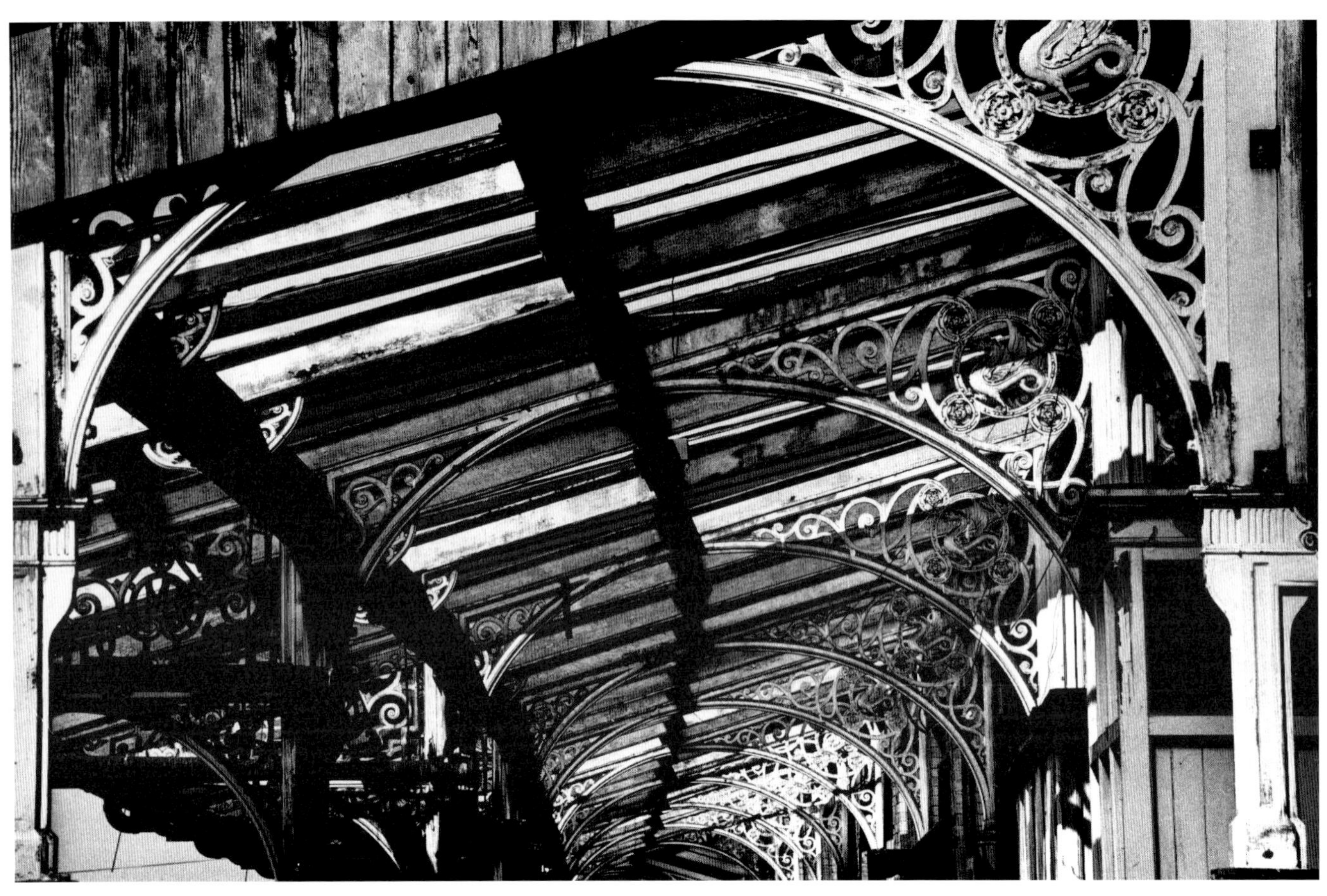

Station roof
Hellifield, Yorkshire

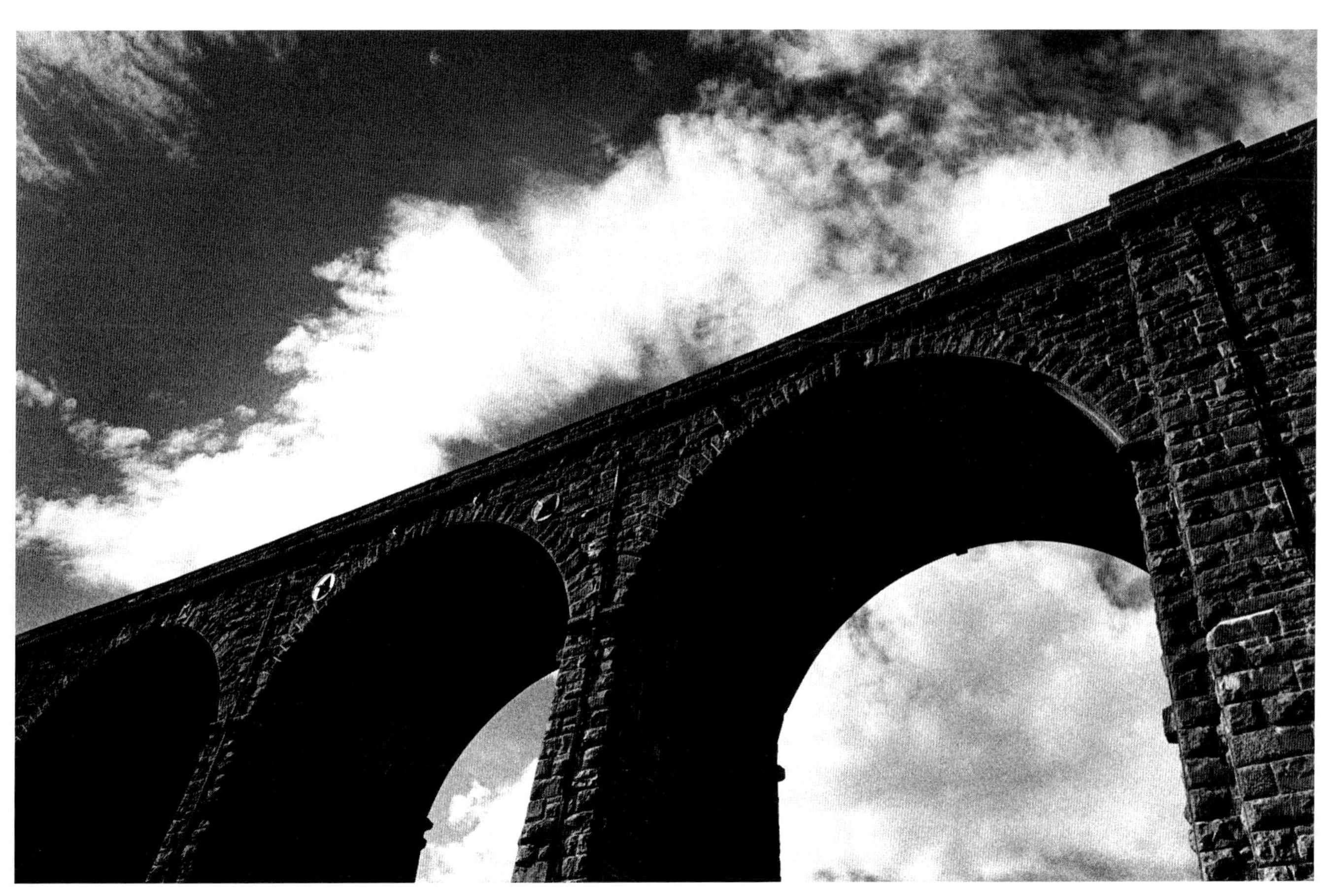

Ribblehead, North Yorkshire

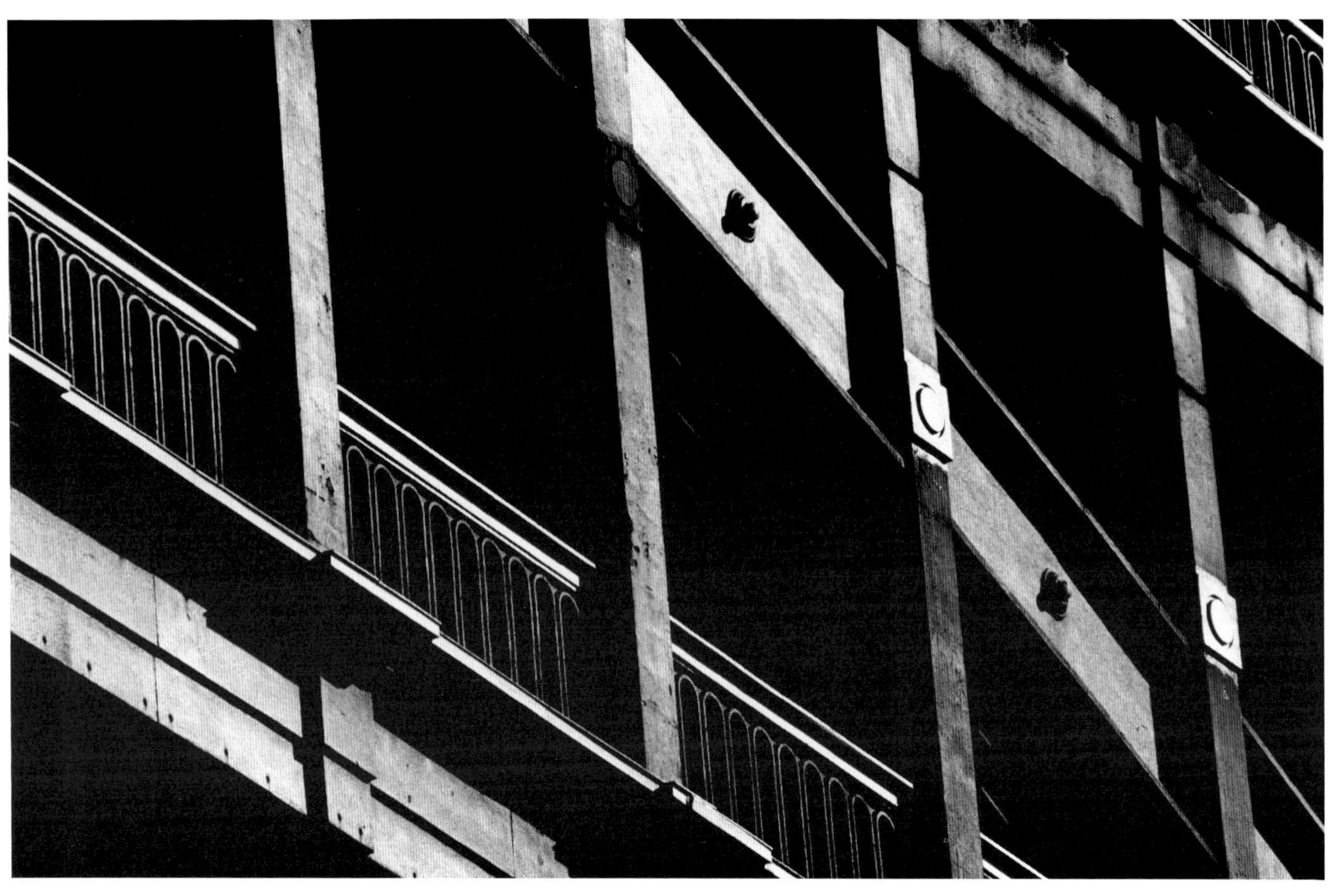

Stephenson's high level bridge
Newcastle

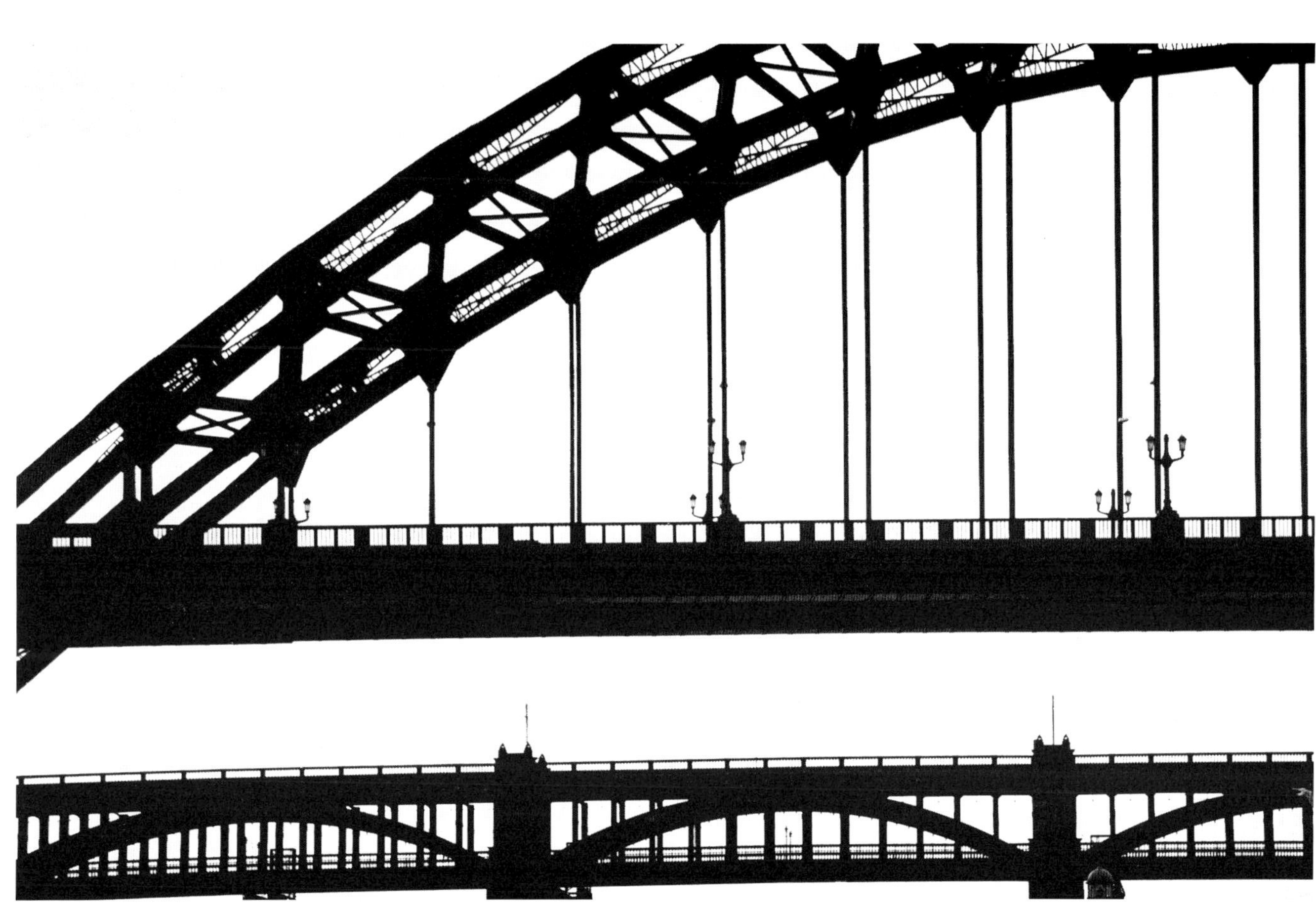

Tyne bridges

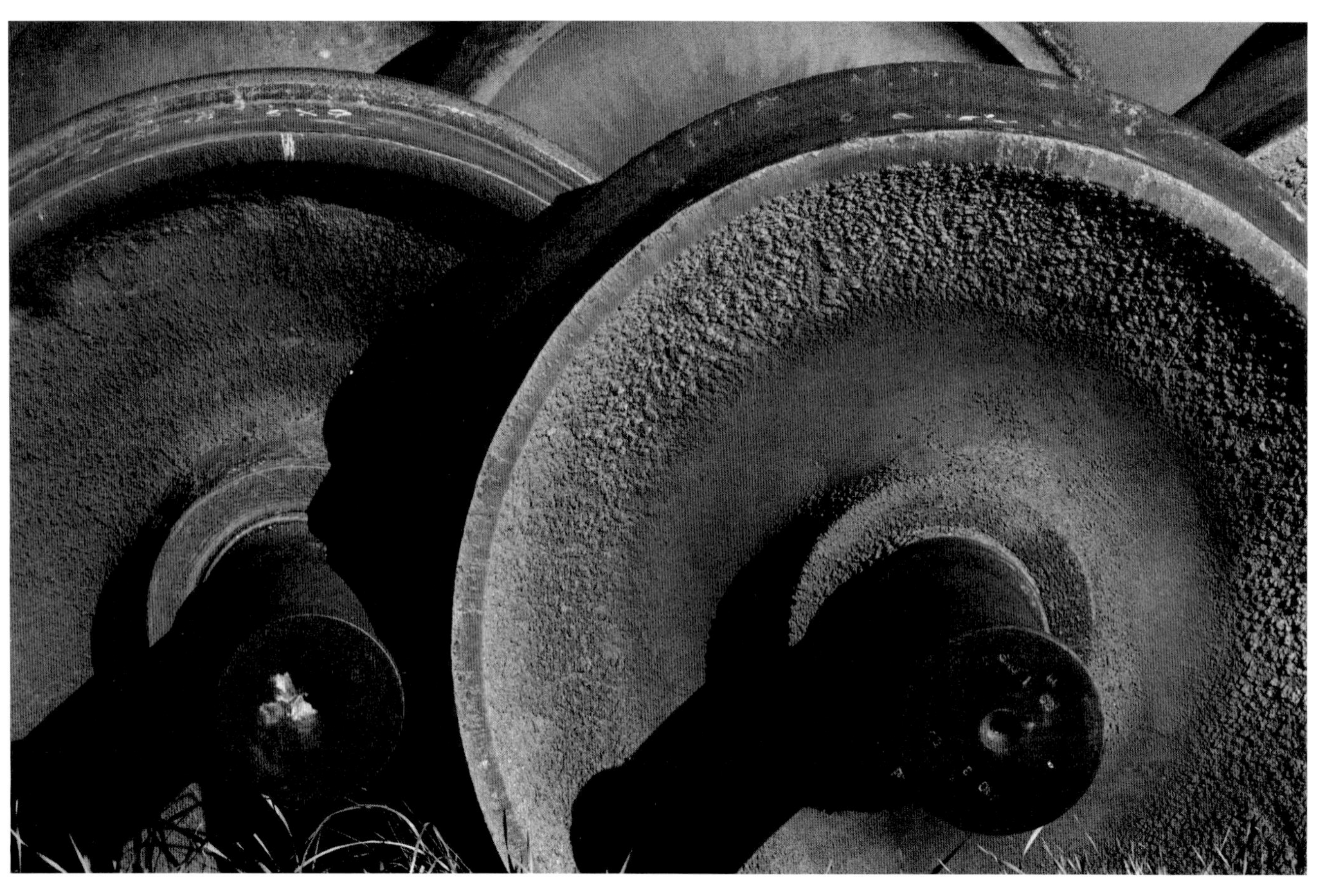

Railway wagon wheels
Jamestown, California

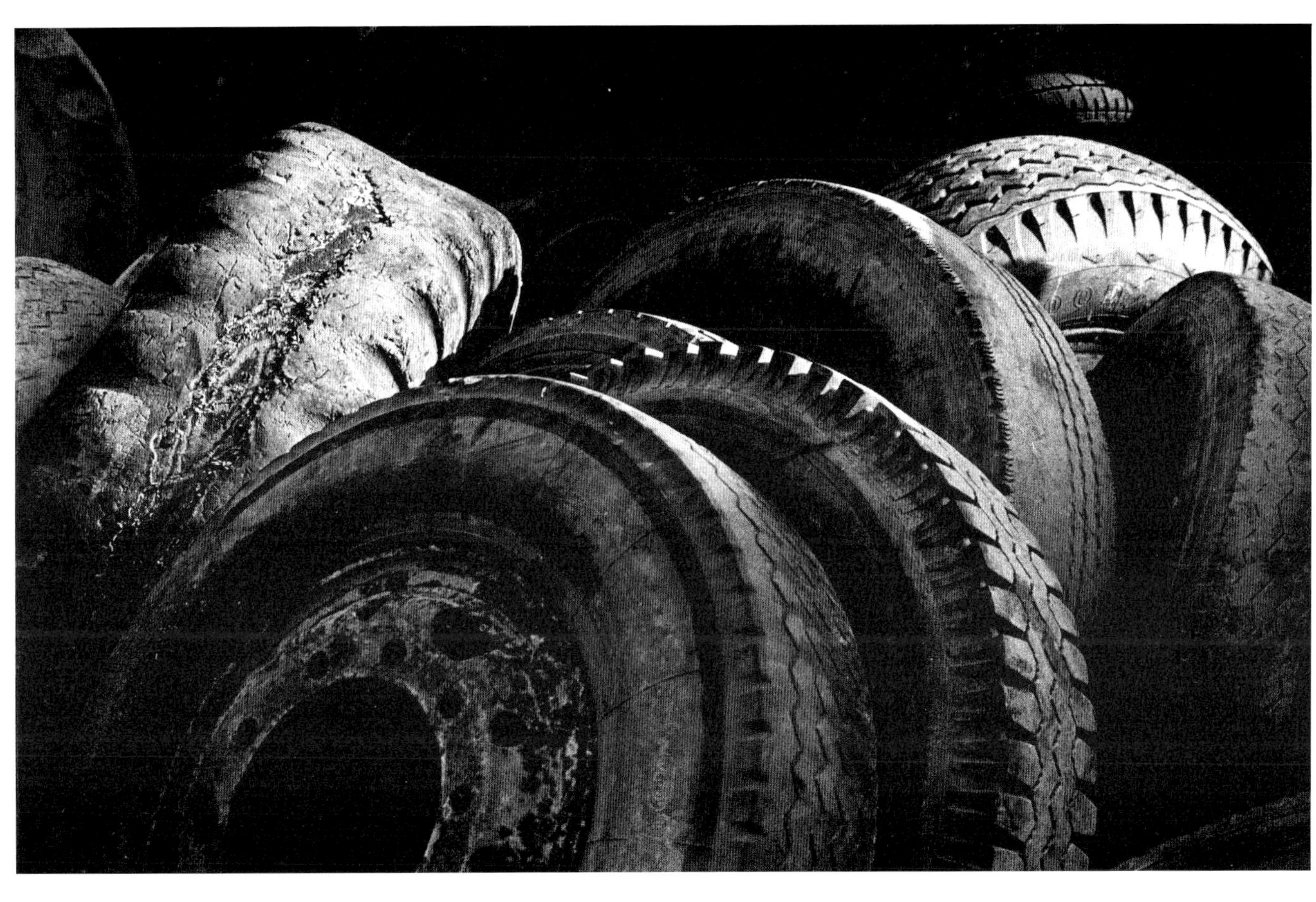

Tyre dump
Llantony Quay, Gloucestershire

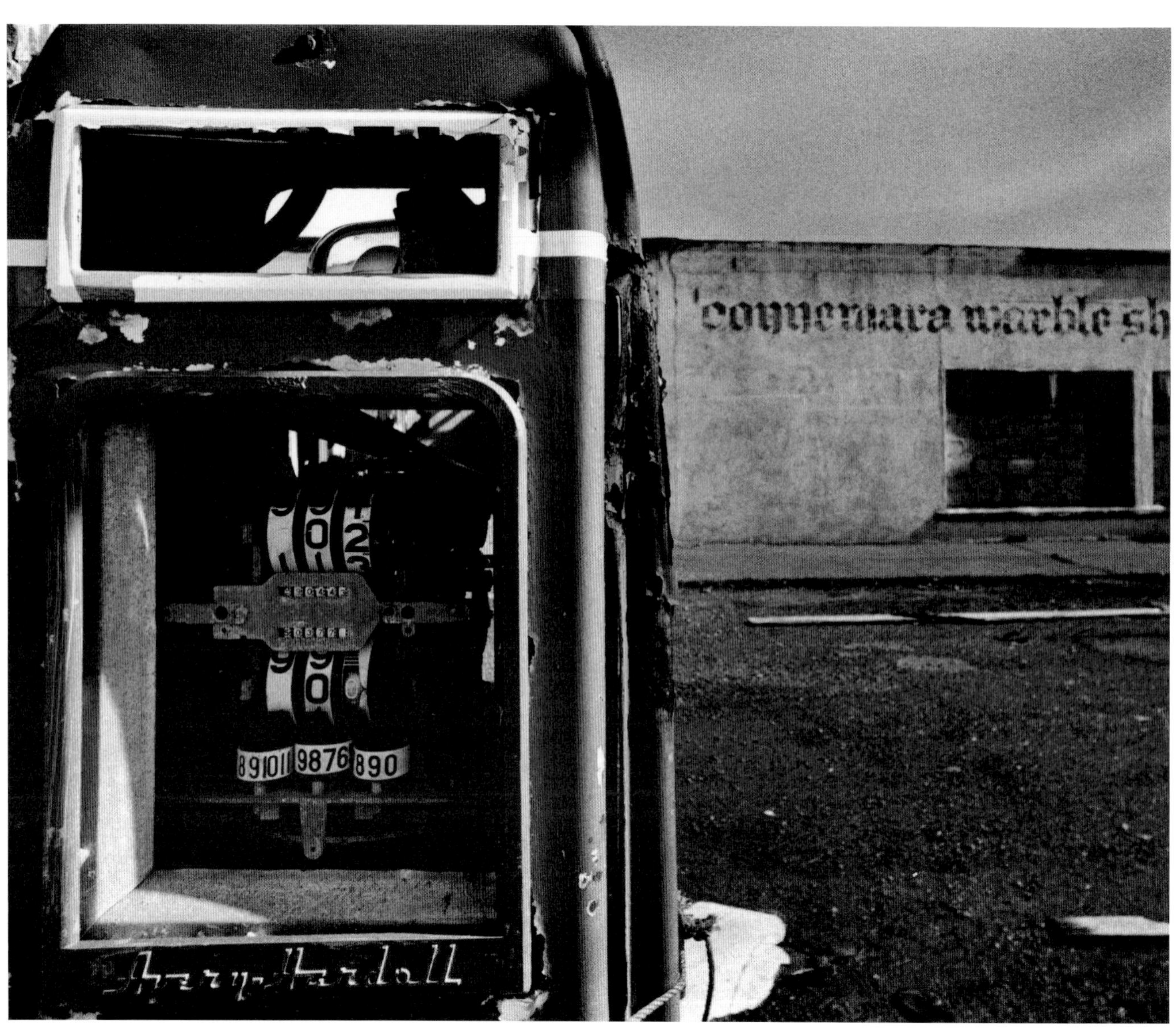

Petrol pump
Connemara, Ireland

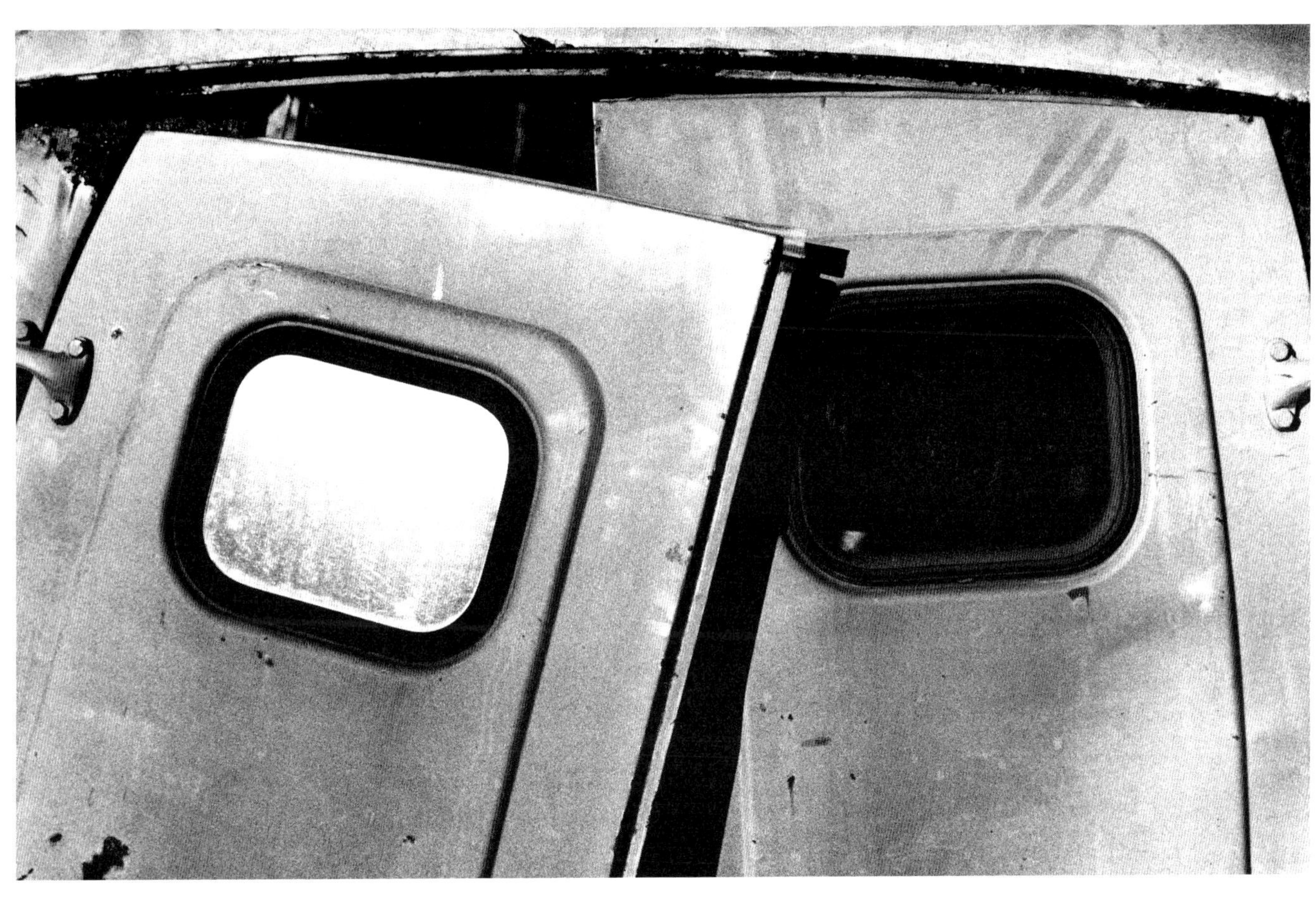

Morris Minor rear doors
Berkeley, Gloucestershire

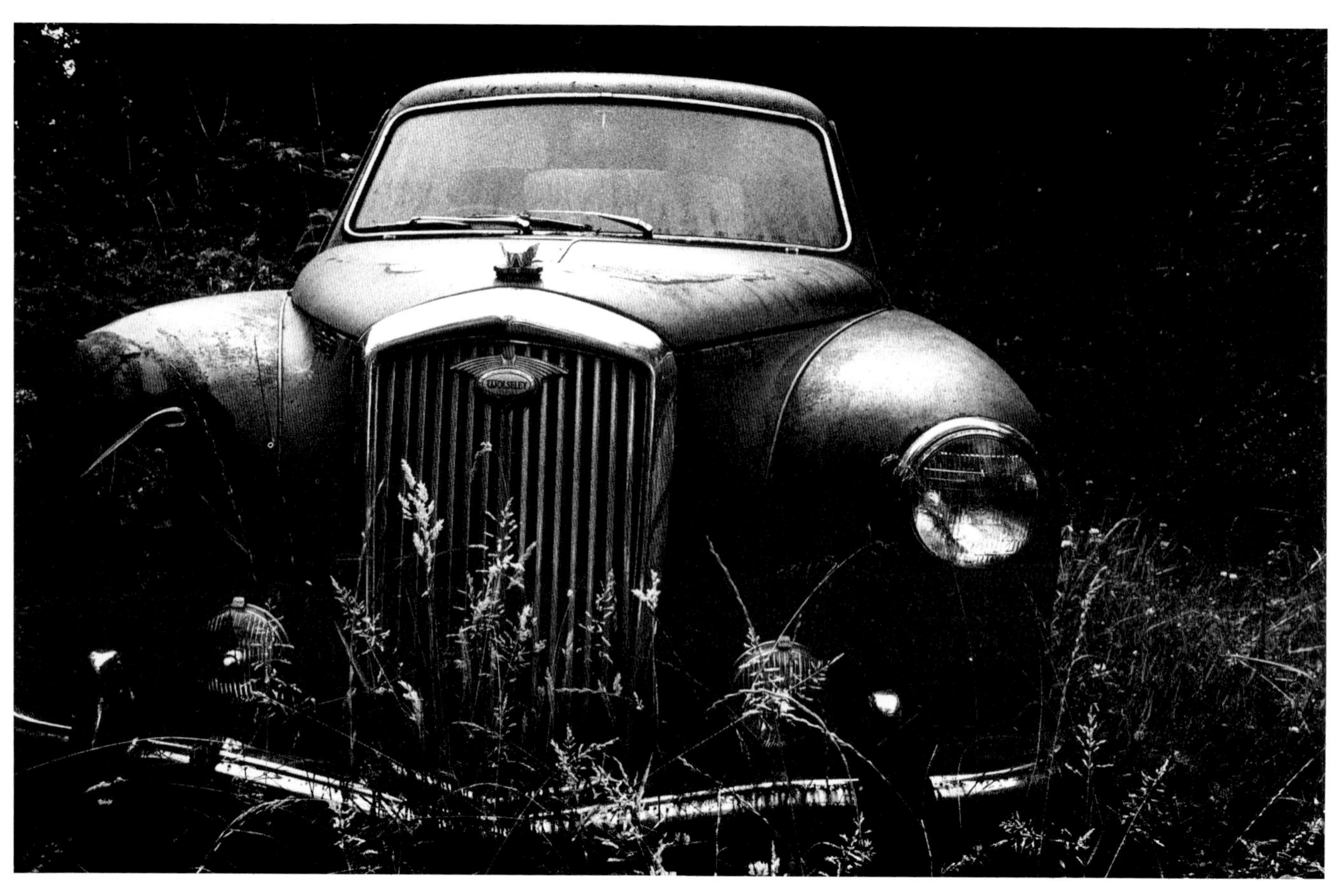

Old Wolseley
Broad Oak, Herefordshire

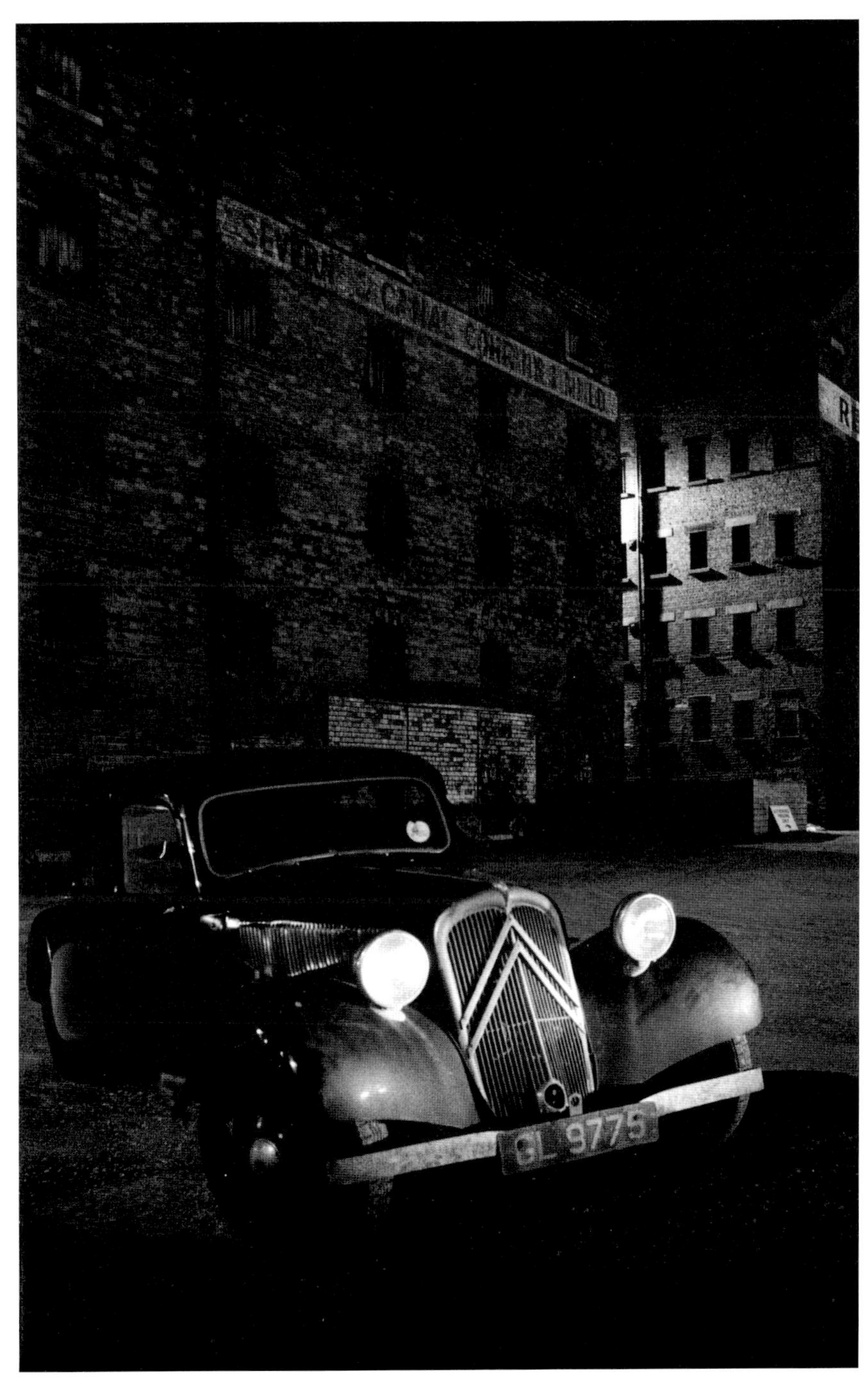

Old Citroen
Gloucester

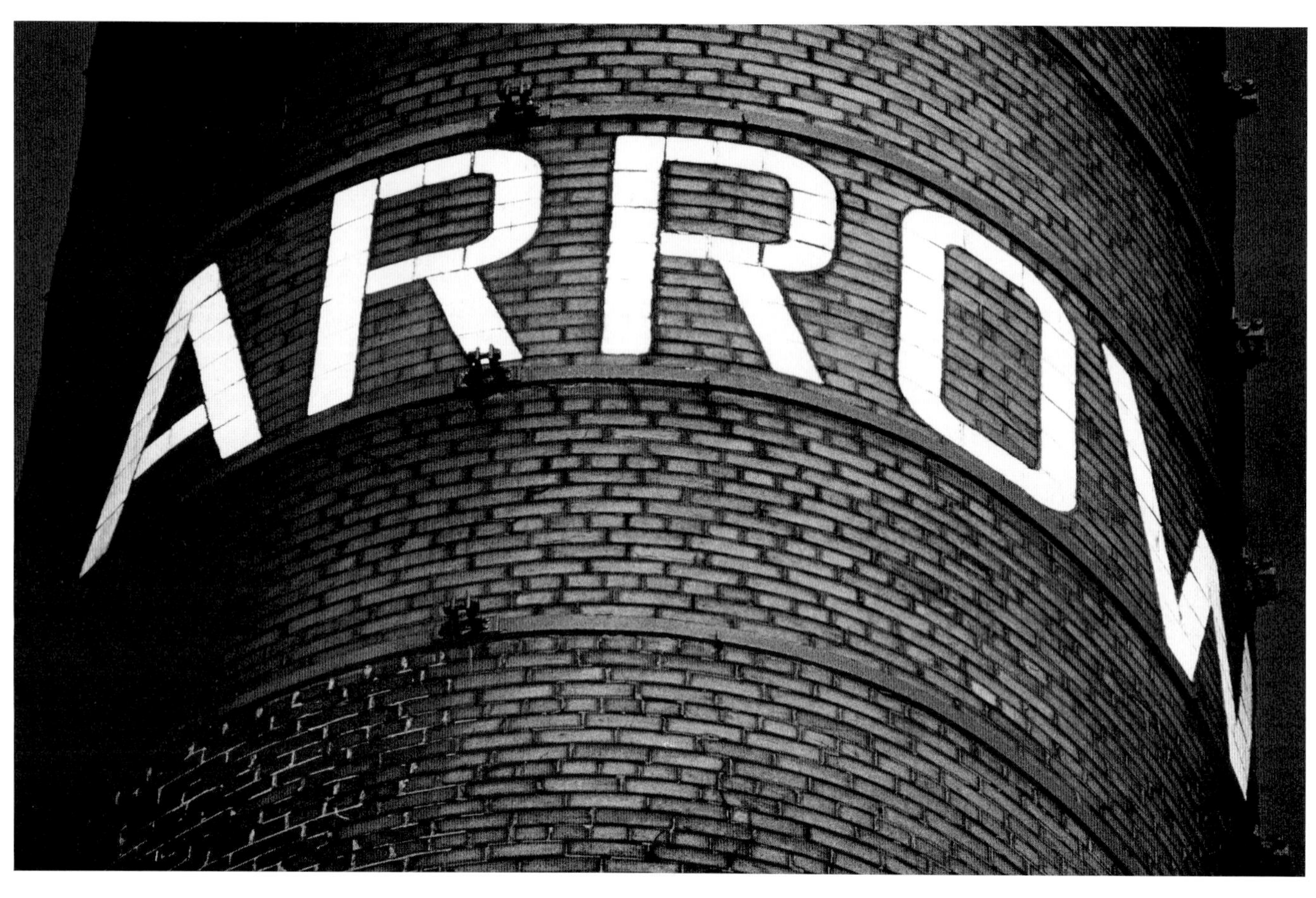

Arrow Mill chimney
Near Rochdale, Lancashire

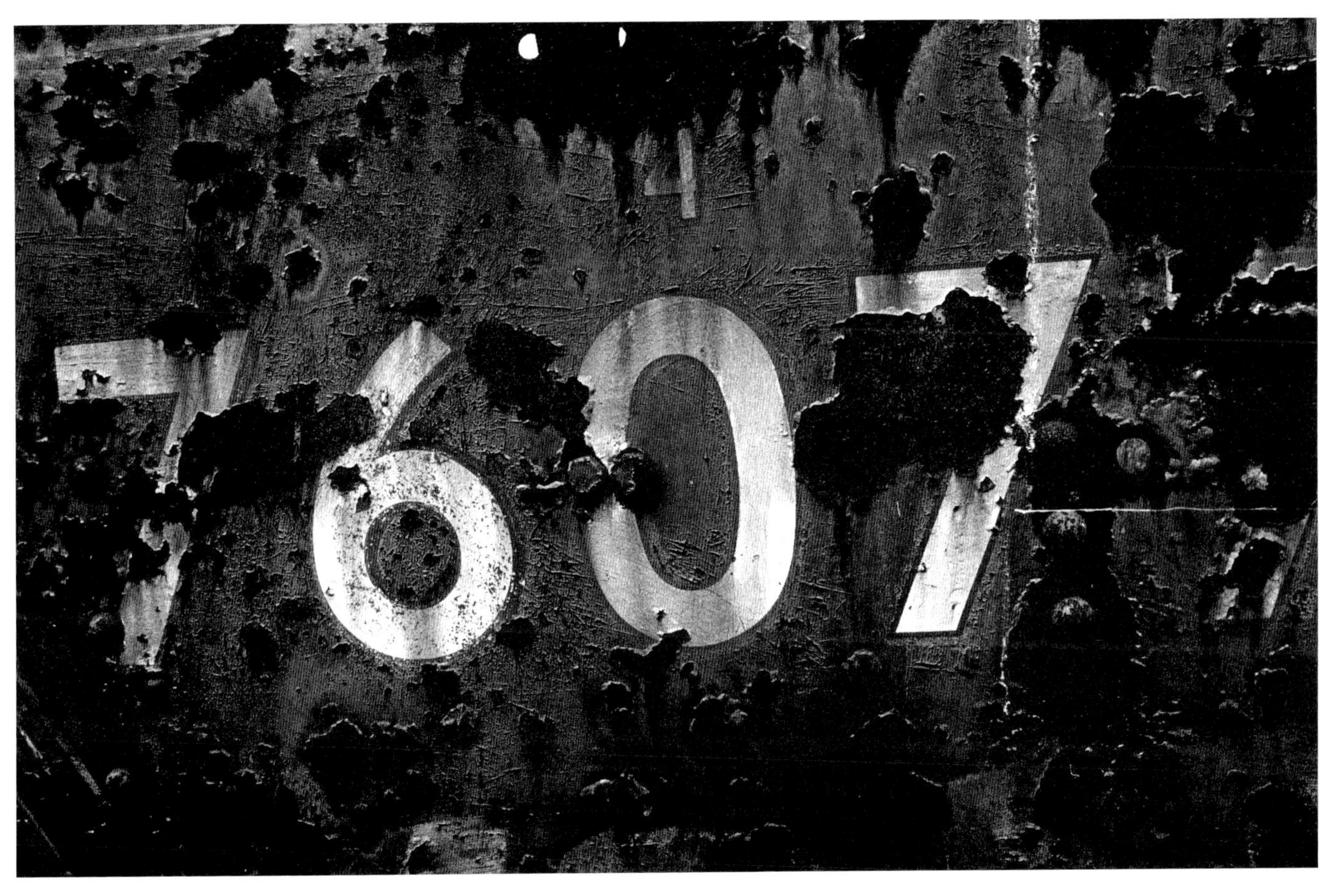

Shadows and rust

Winchcombe, Gloucestershire

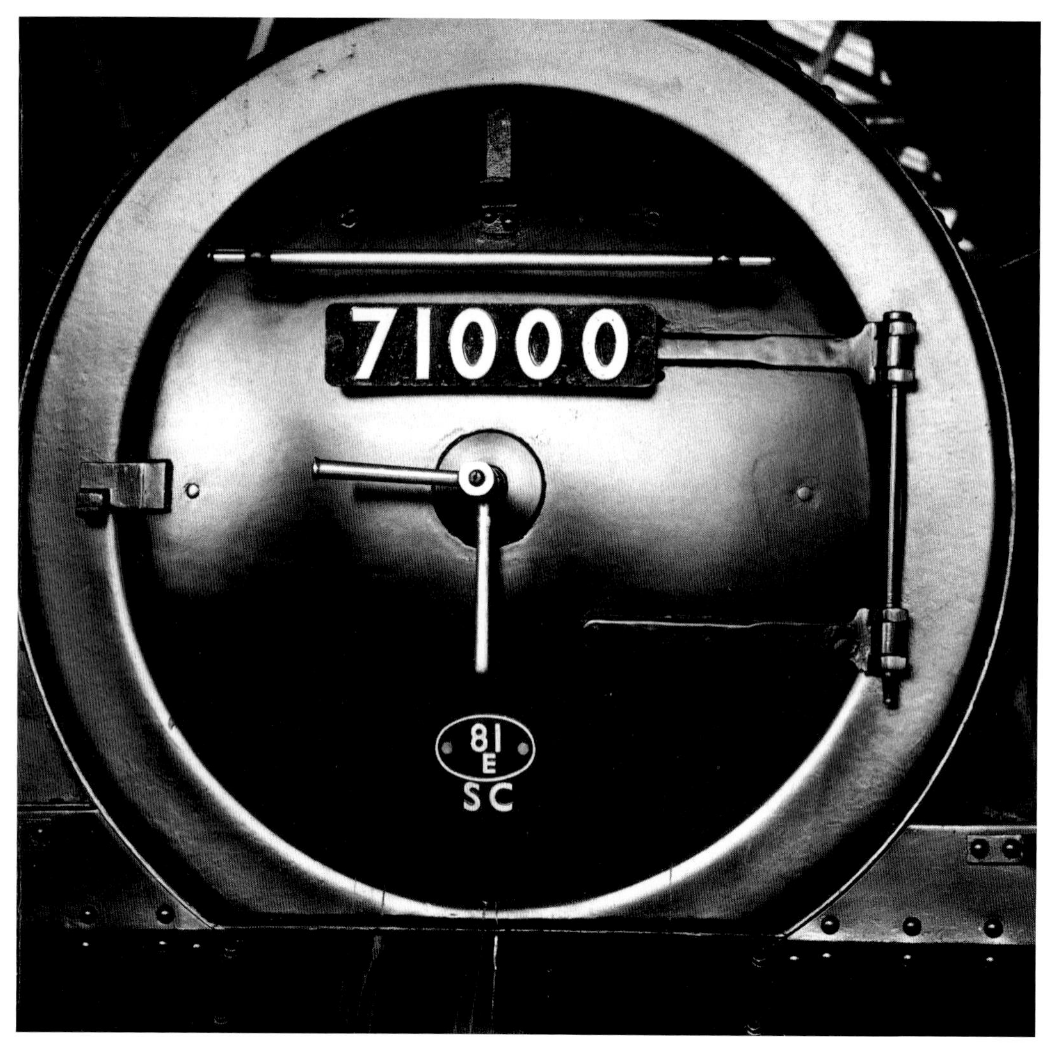

71000

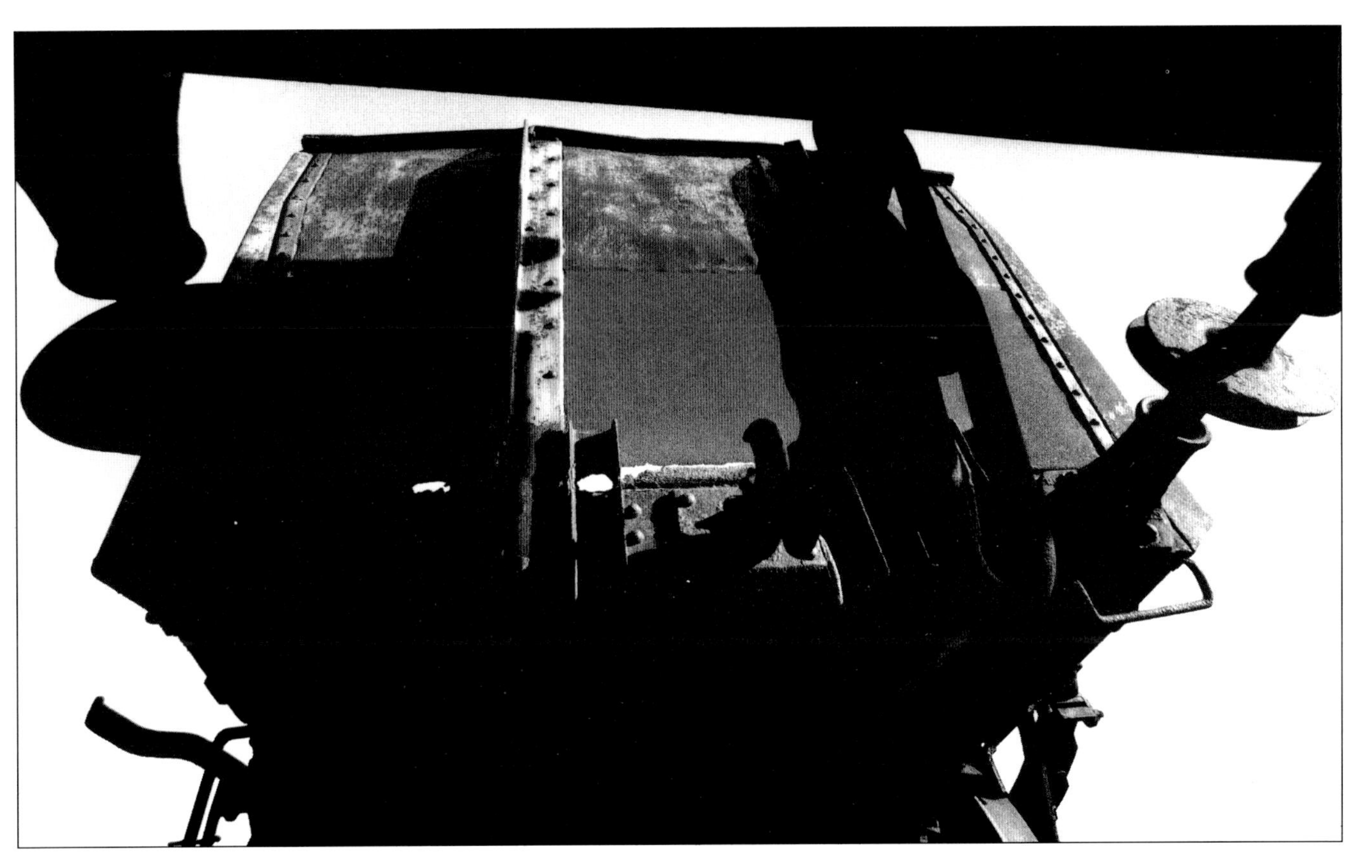

Coal wagon
Sharpness, Gloucestershire

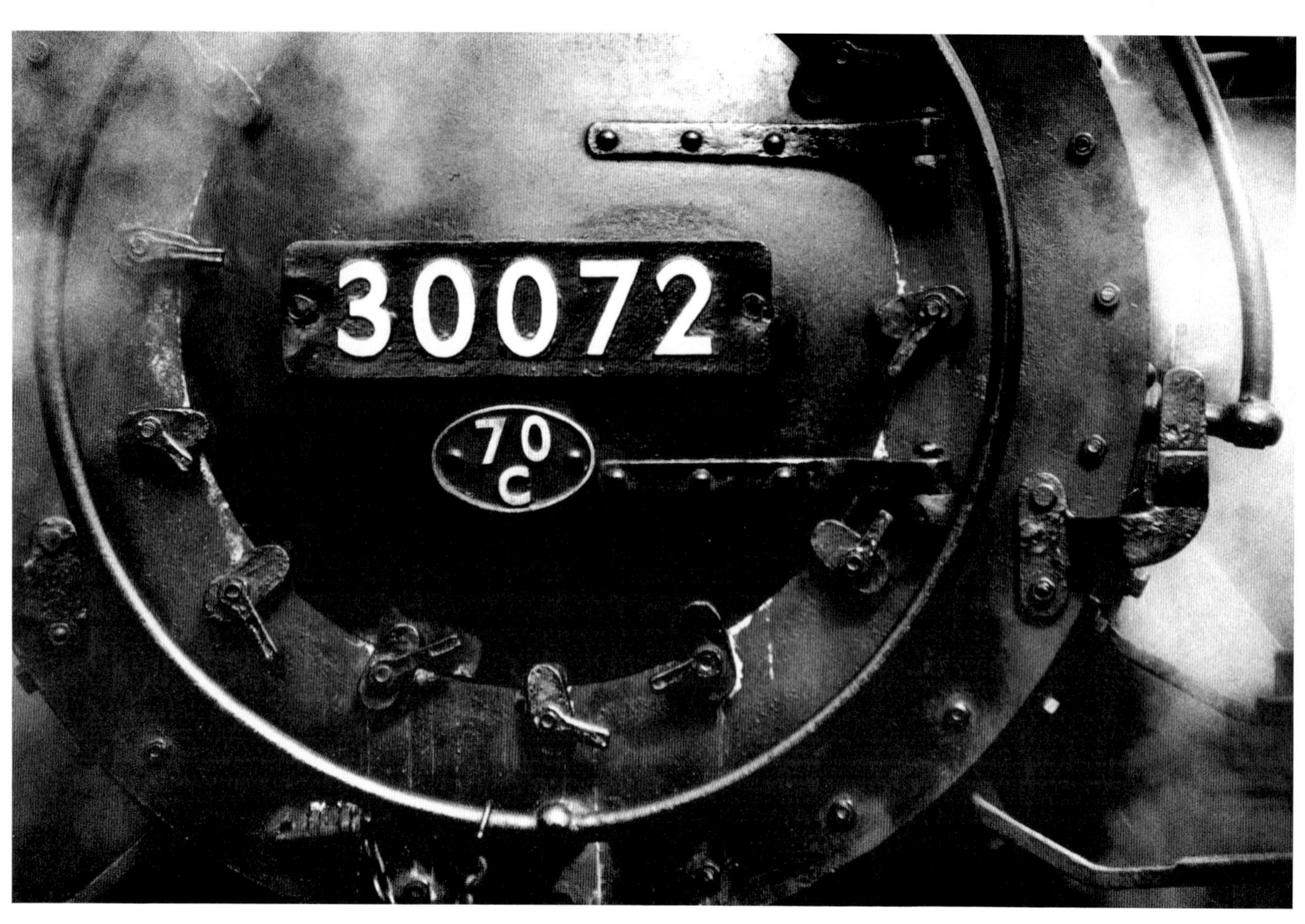

30072

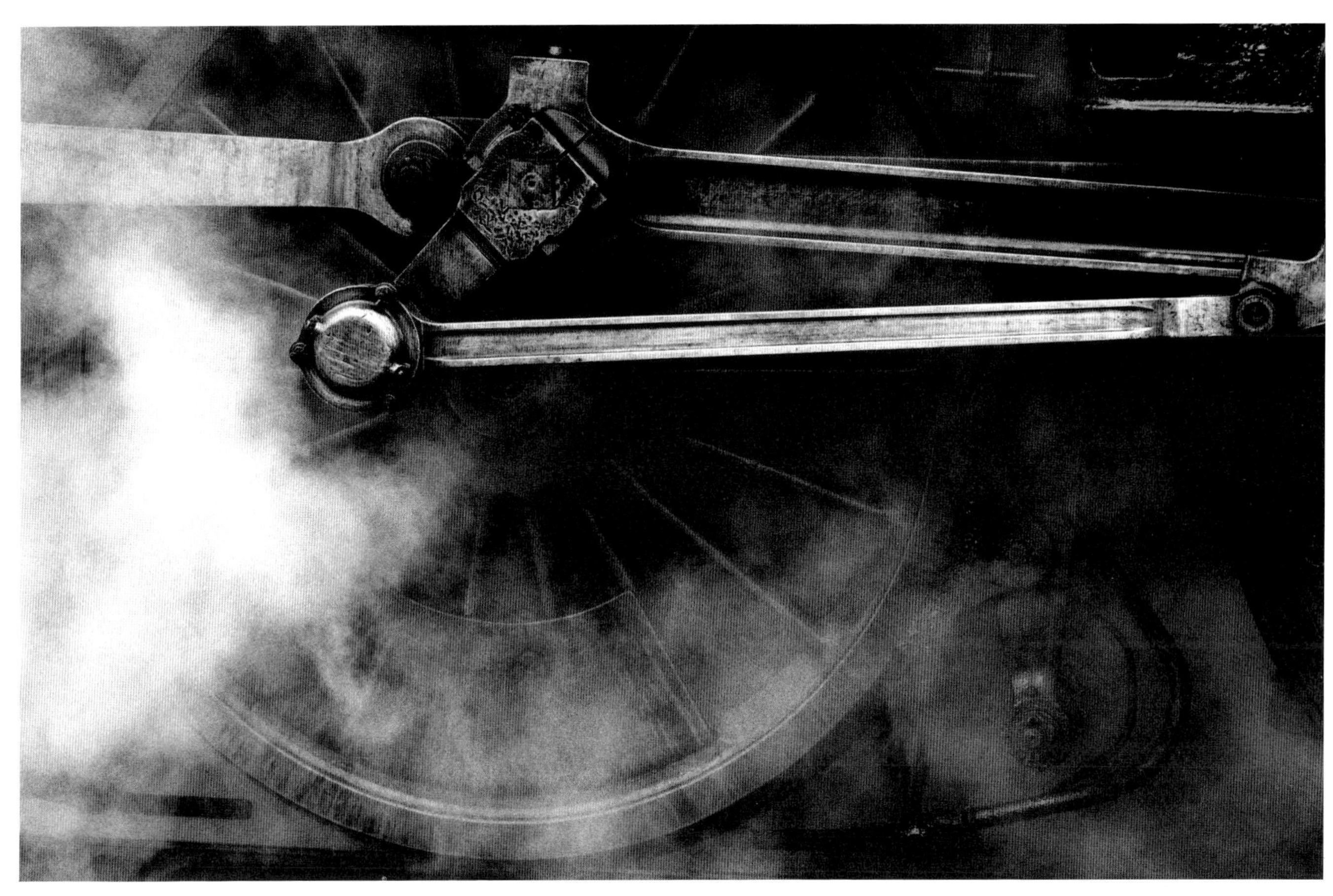

Locomotive wheel
Kidderminster

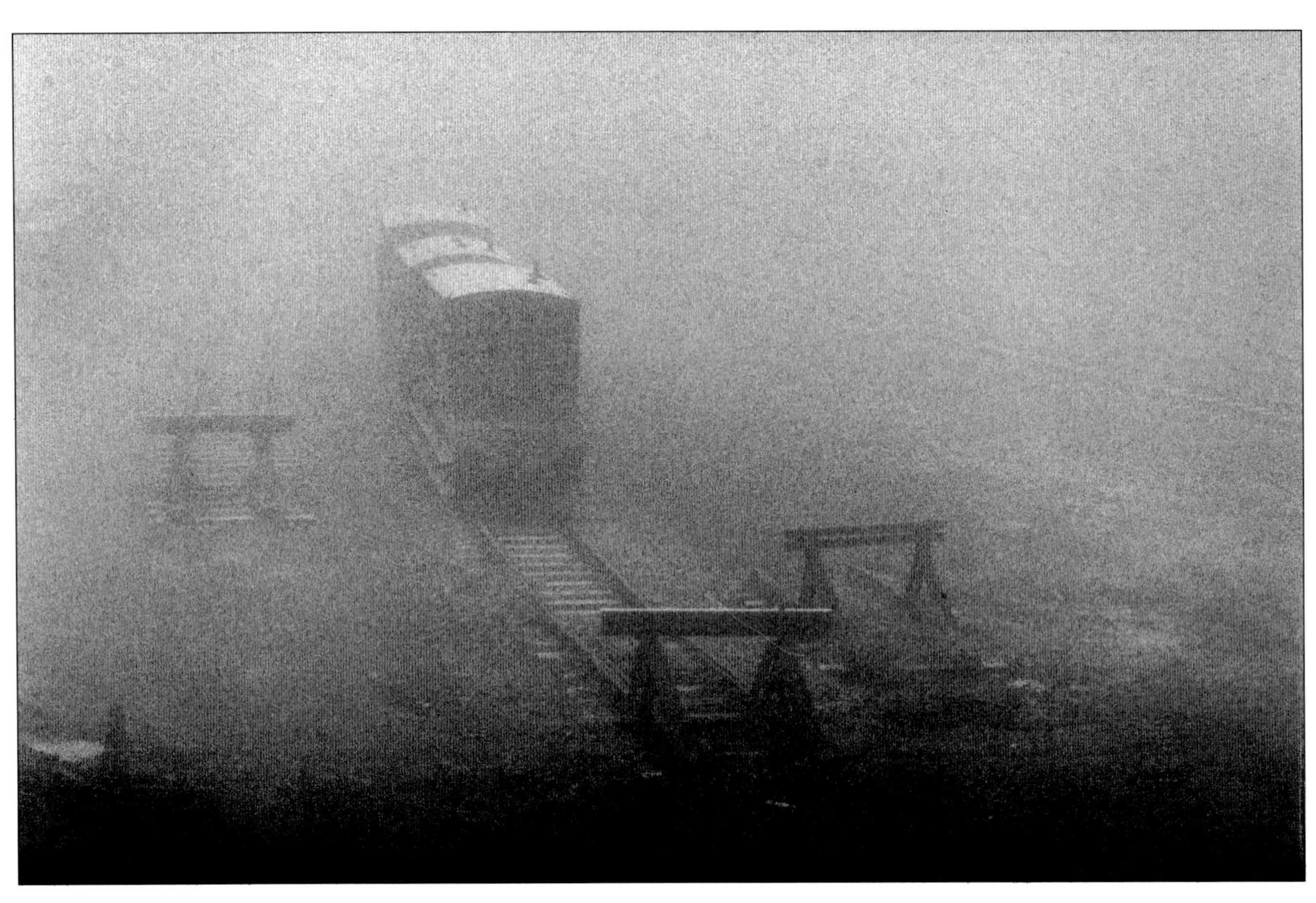

Foggy evening
Railway yards, Gloucester

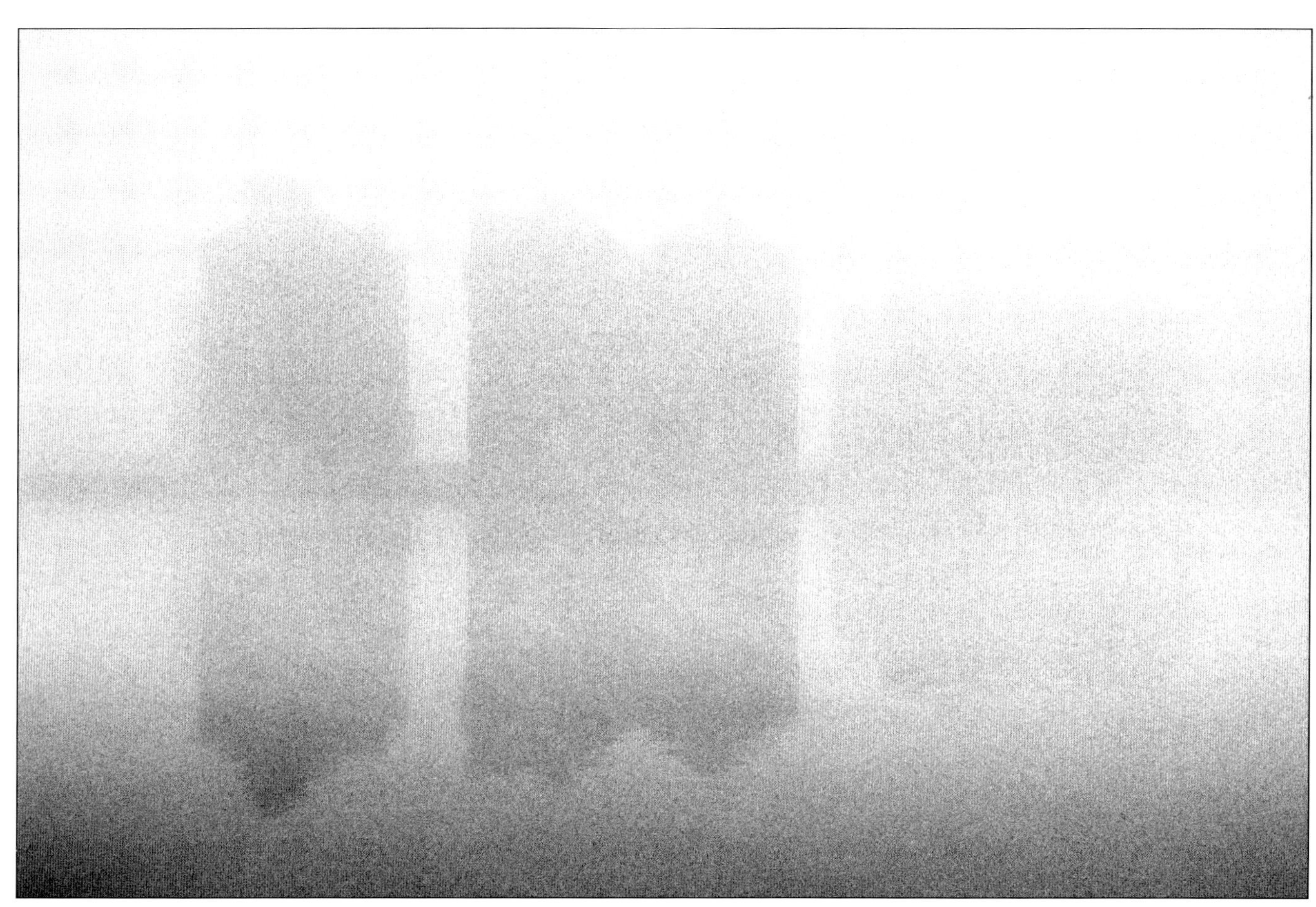

Early morning mist
Gloucester docks

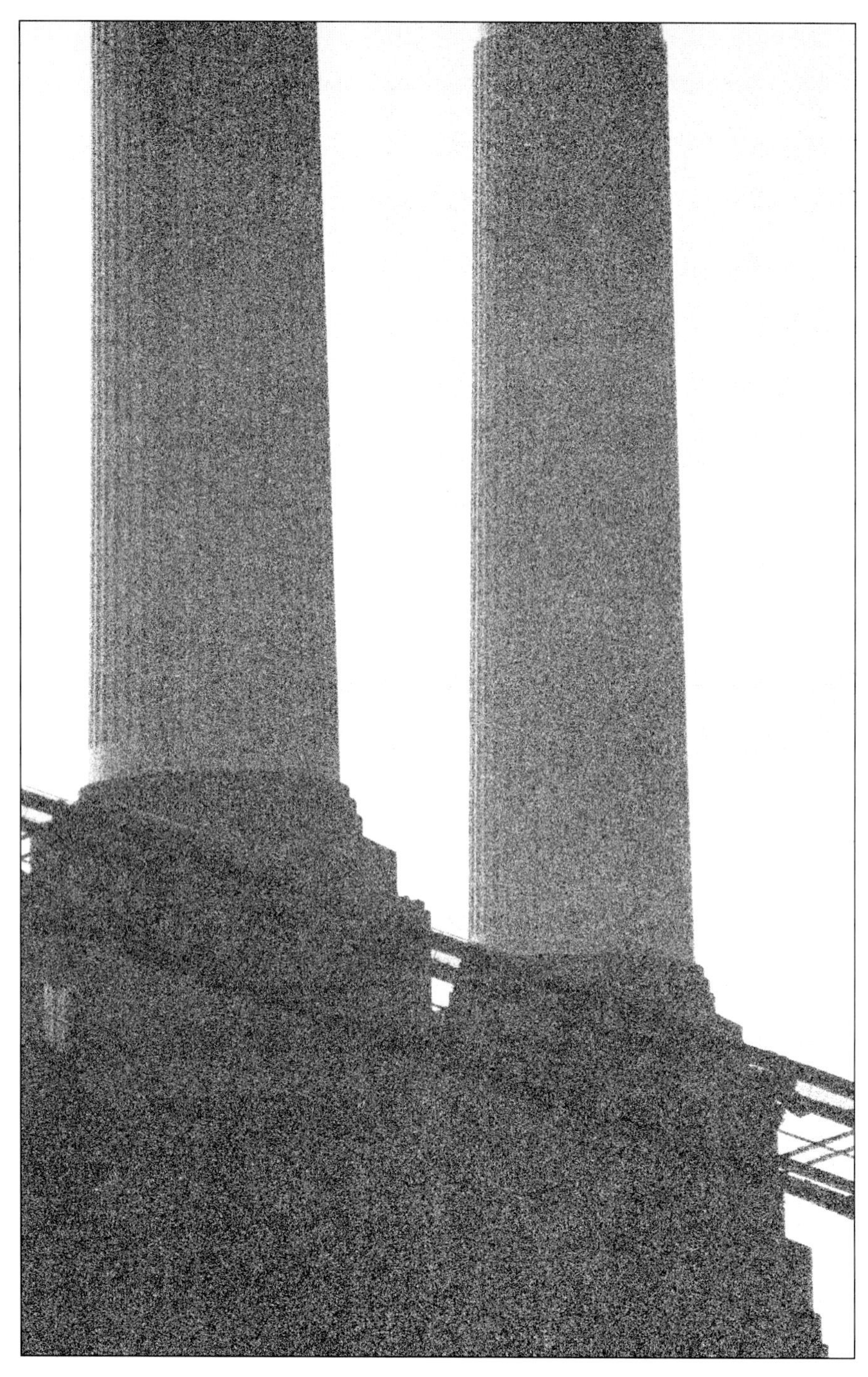

Power station
Battersea, London

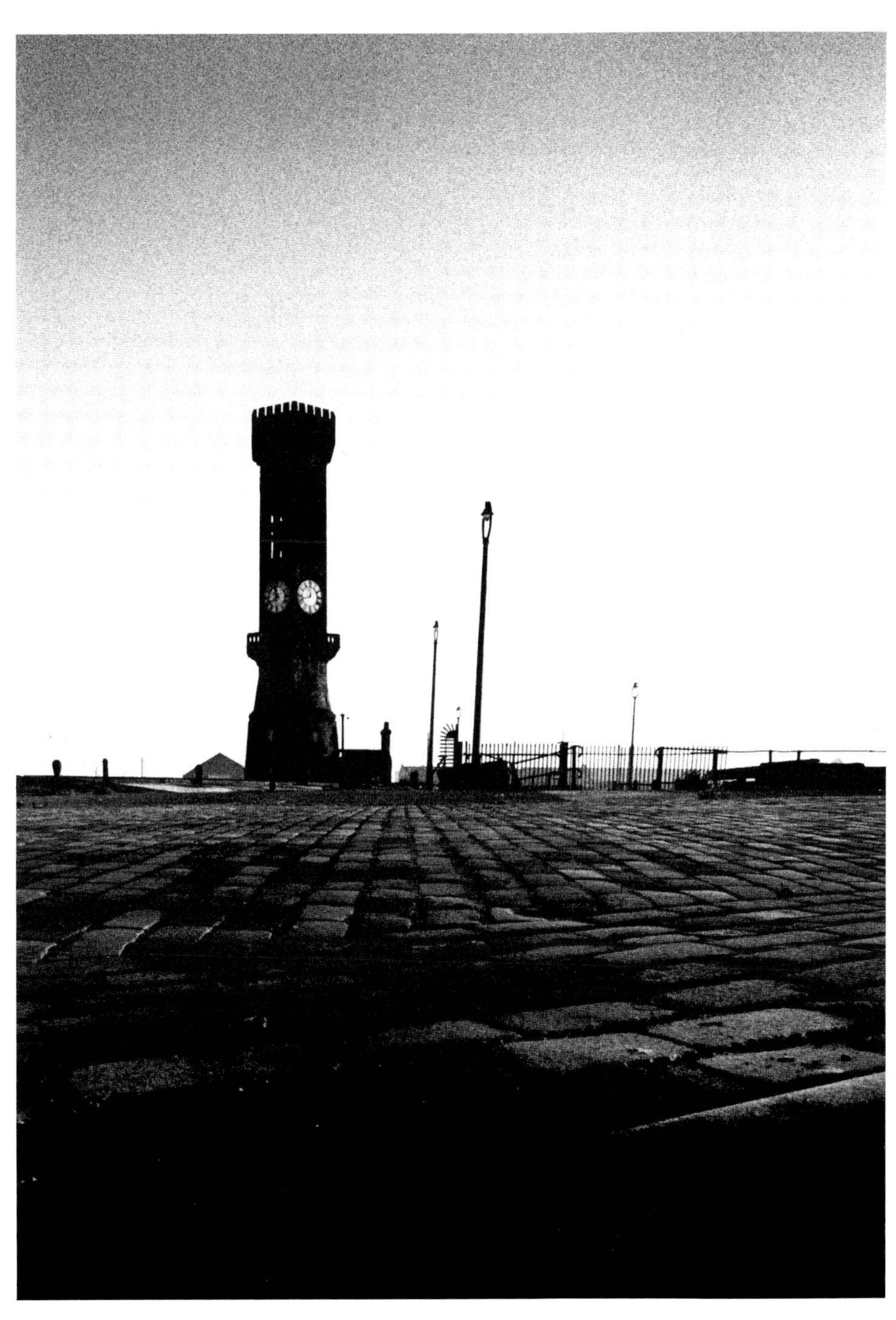

Clock tower
North docks, Liverpool

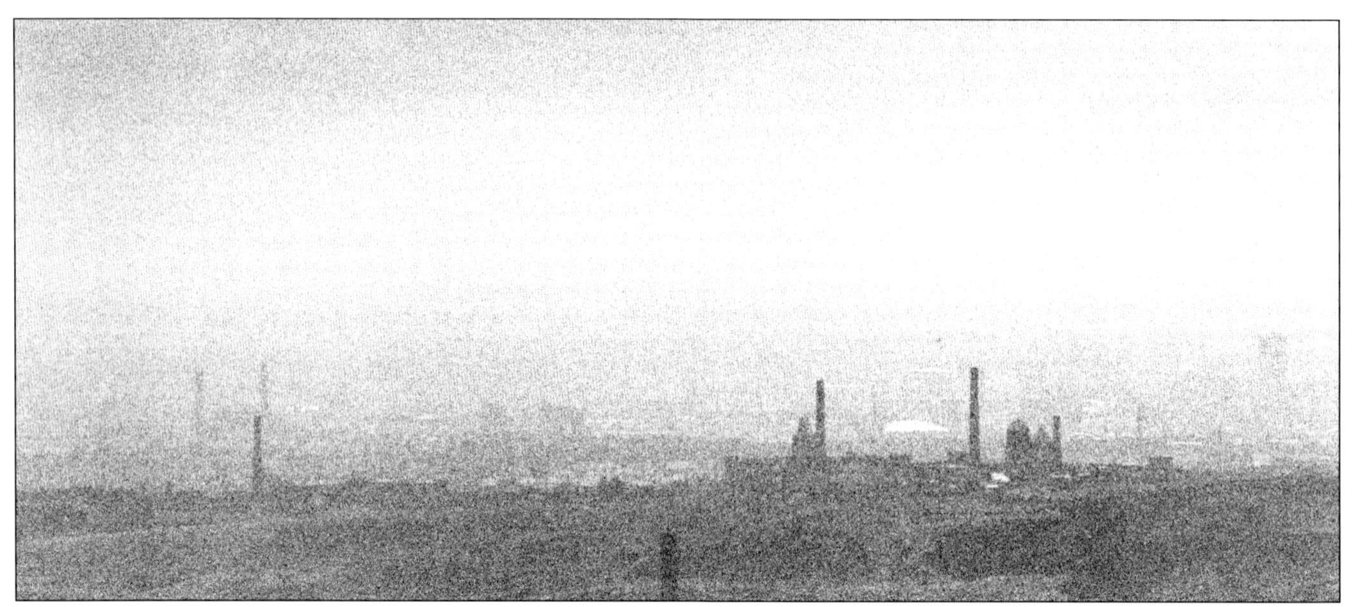

View towards Chadderton
From Scouthead, Greater Manchester

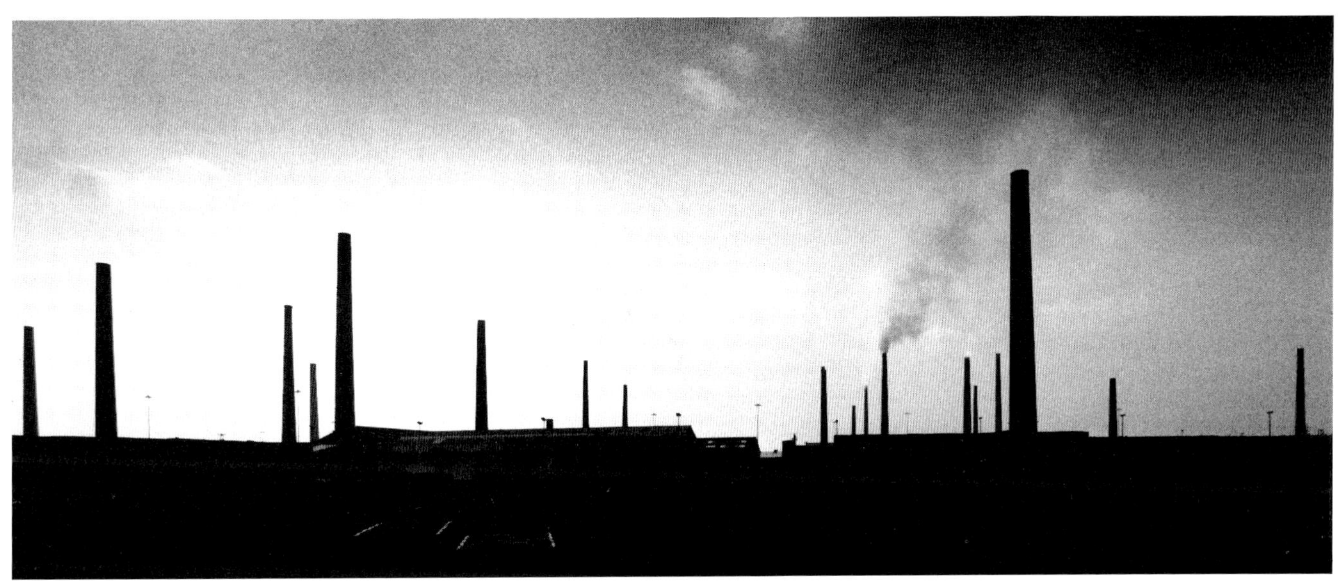

London Brick Company chimneys
Stewartby, Bedfordshire

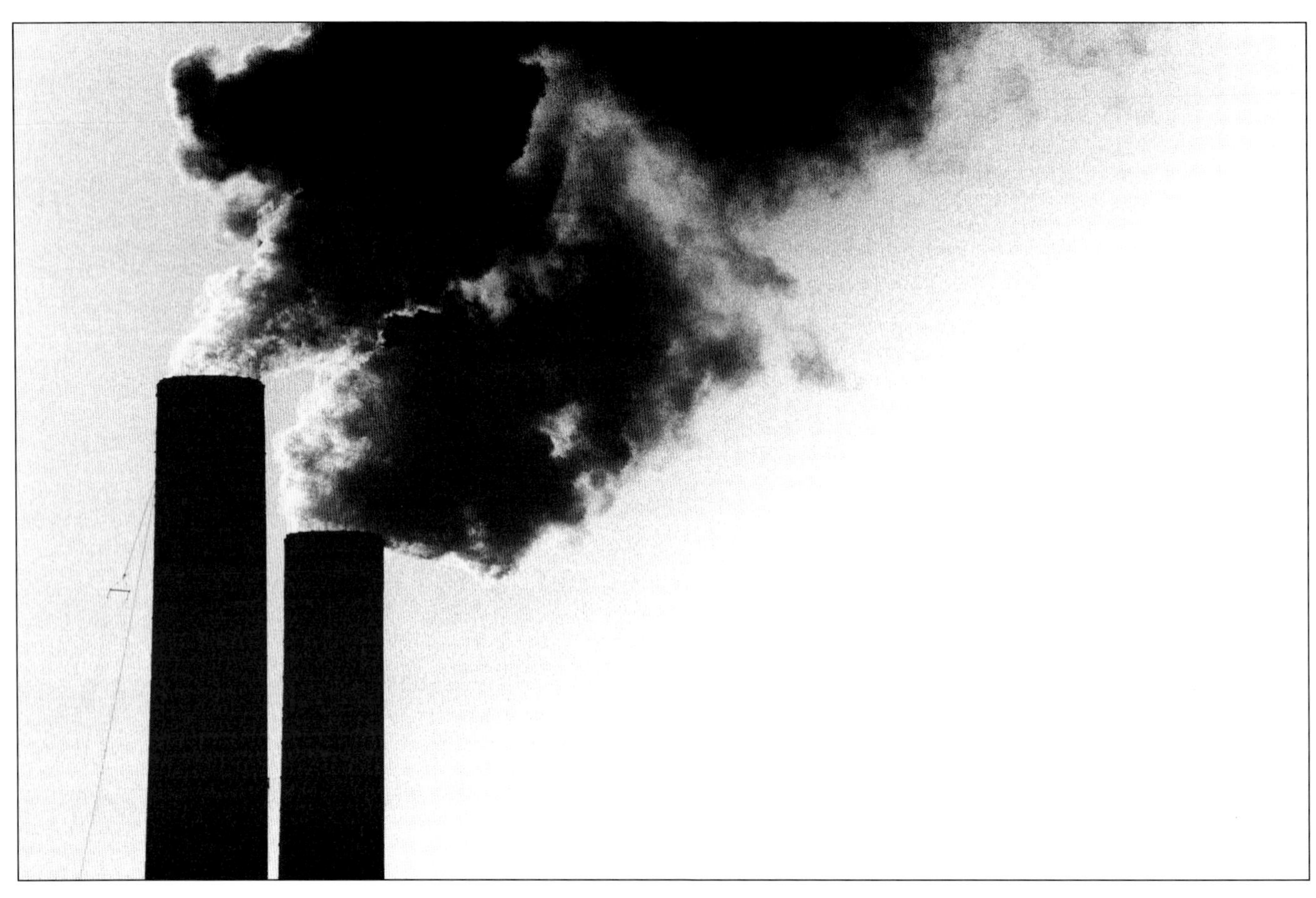

Flour mills
Chelsea, London

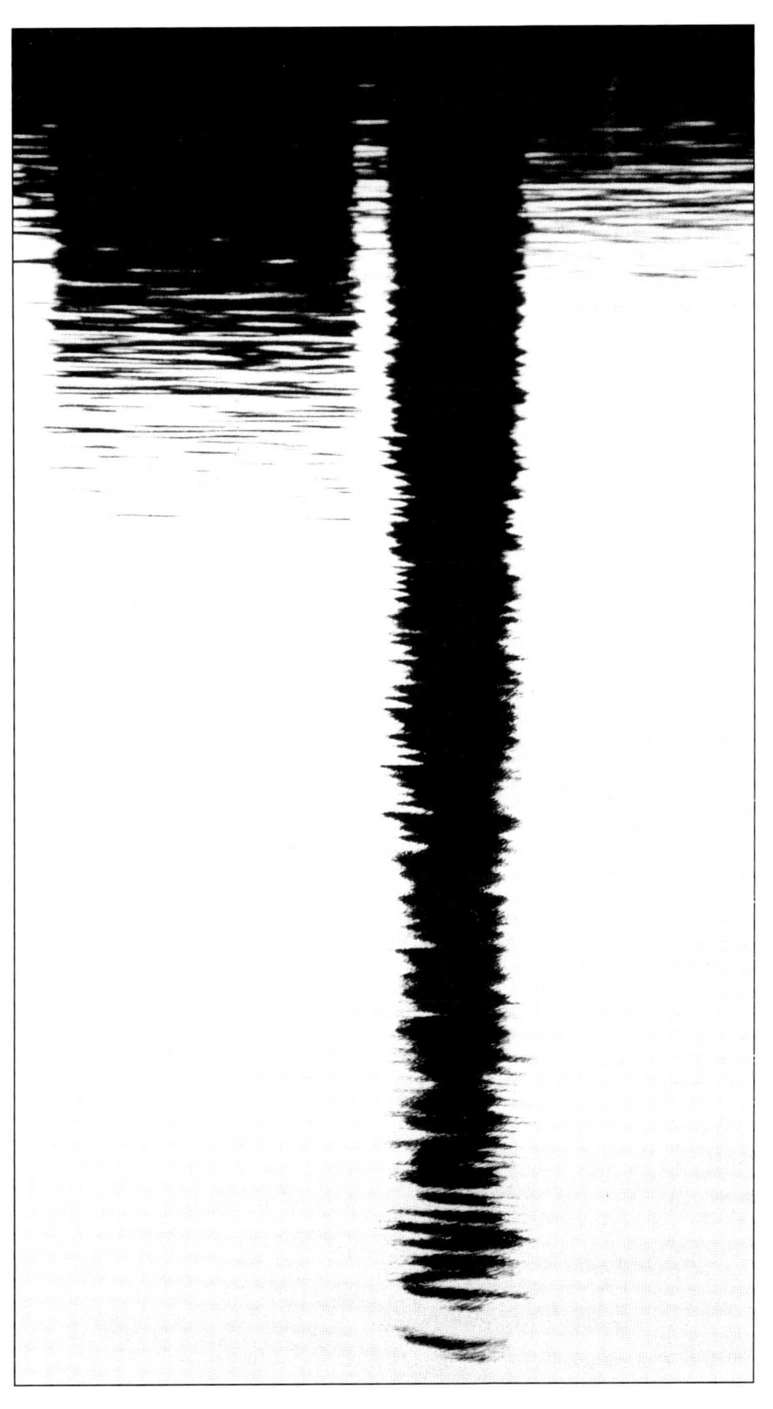

Dock chimney reflection
Liverpool

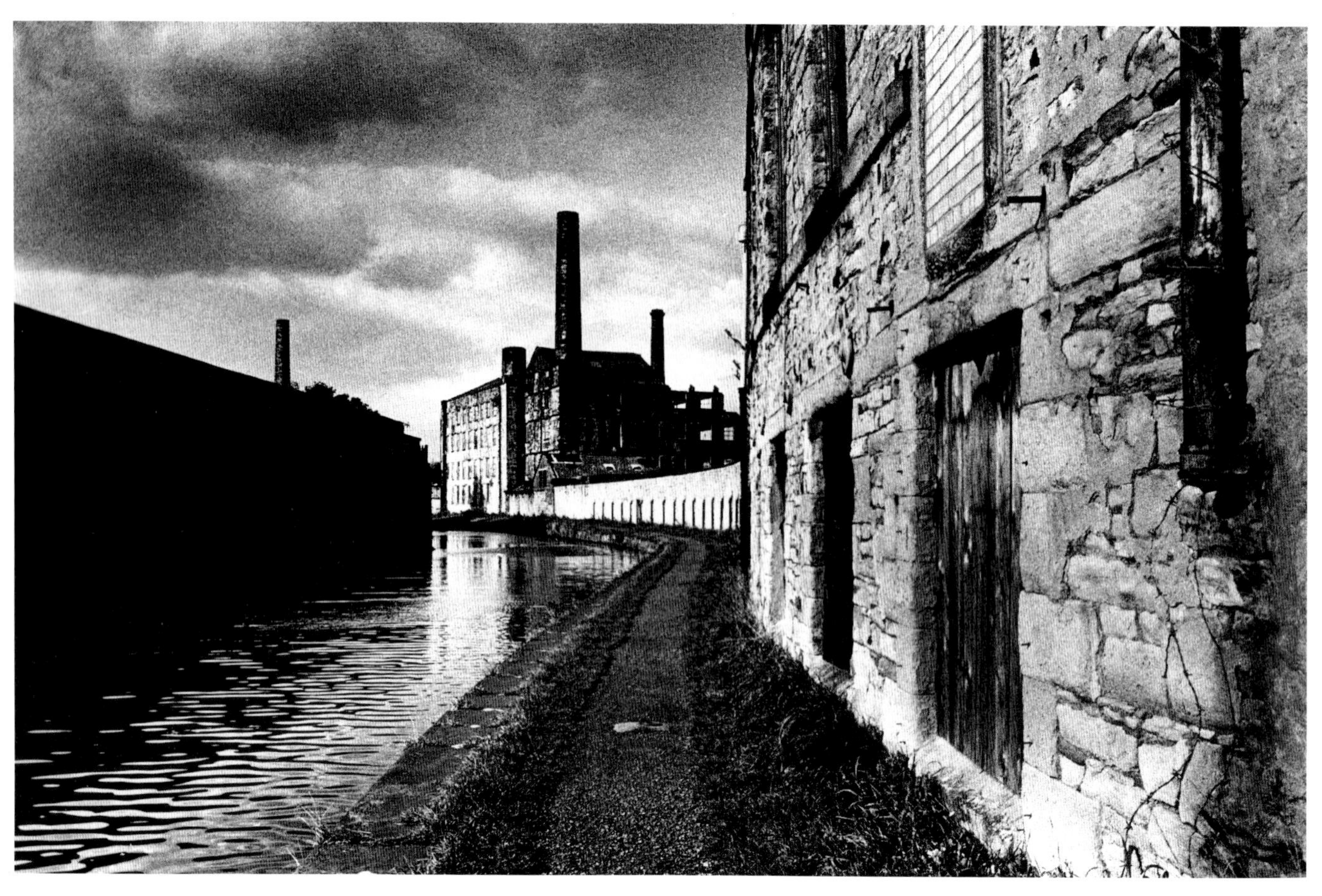

Weavers Triangle
Burnley, Lancashire

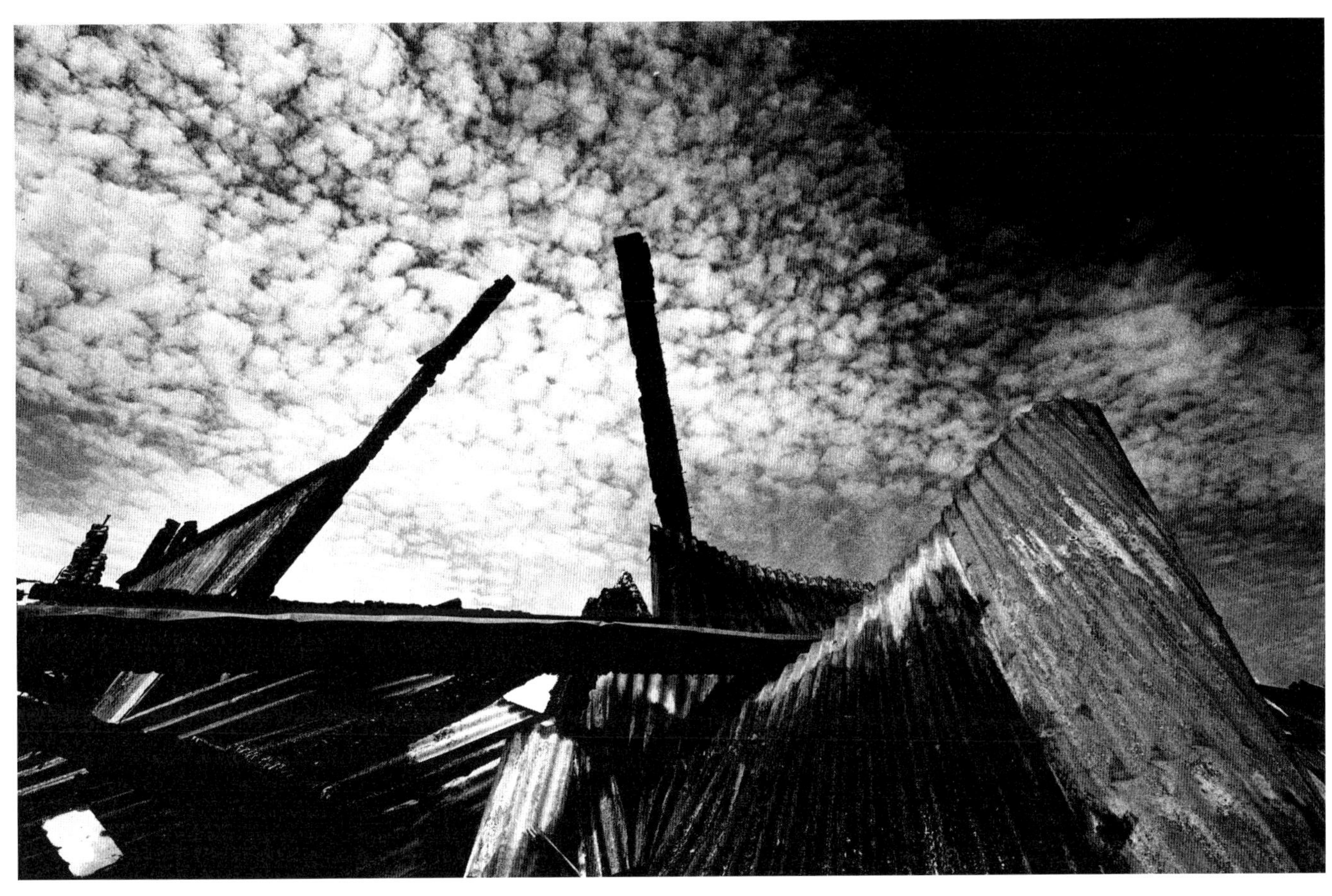

Burnt-out workshop
Aberystwyth, Wales

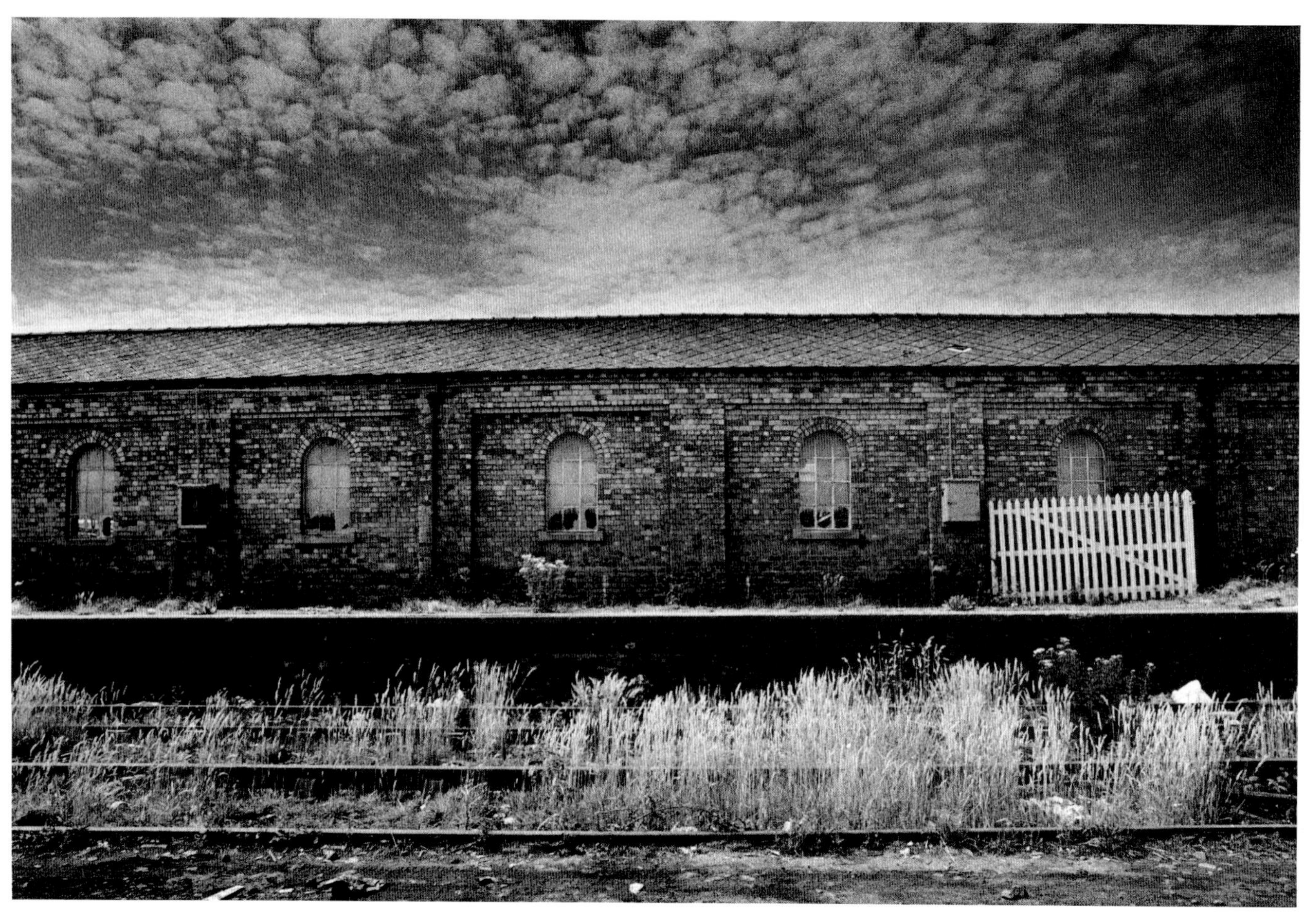

Semi-derelict railway buildings
Wales

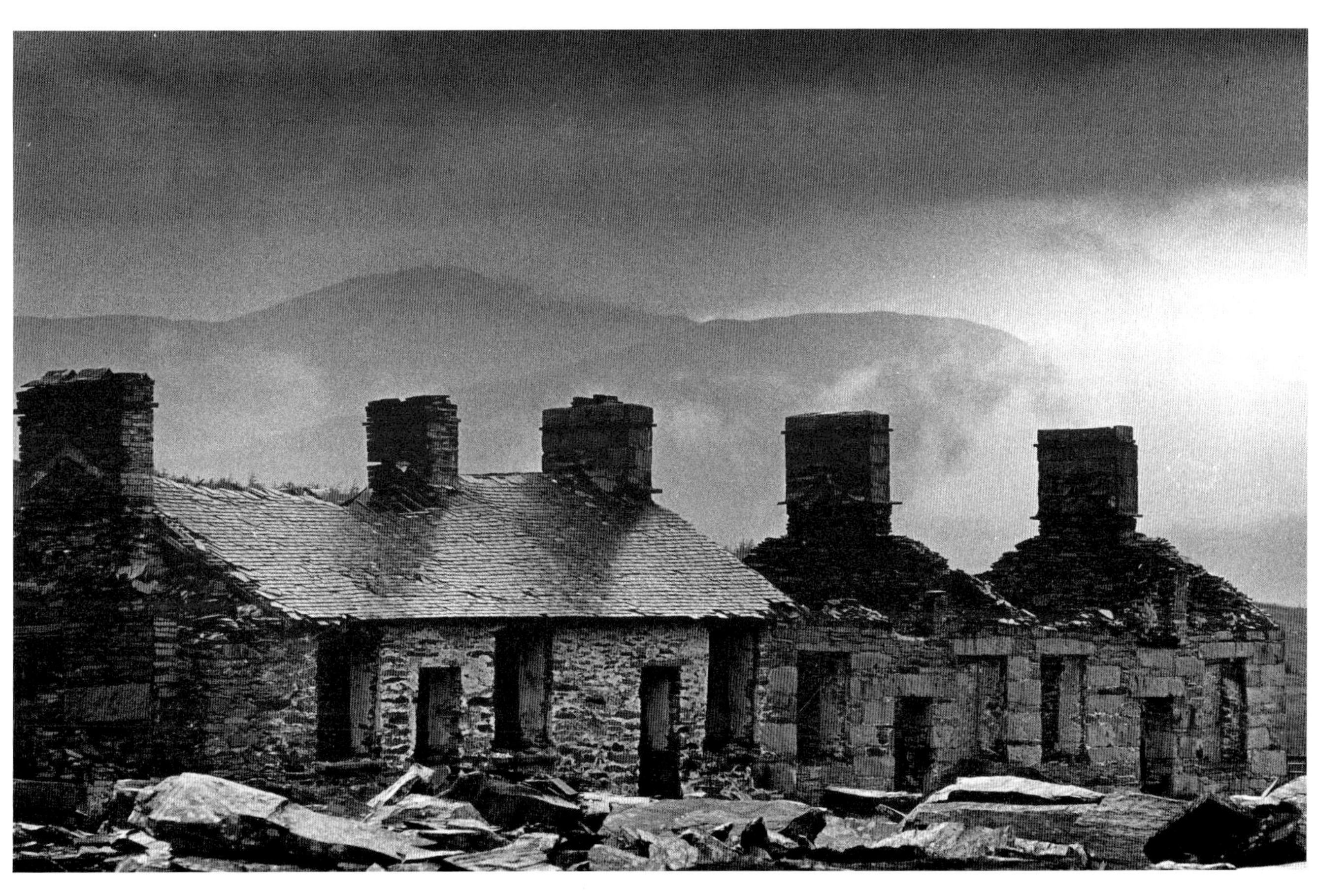

Slate grey
Near Capel Curig, North Wales

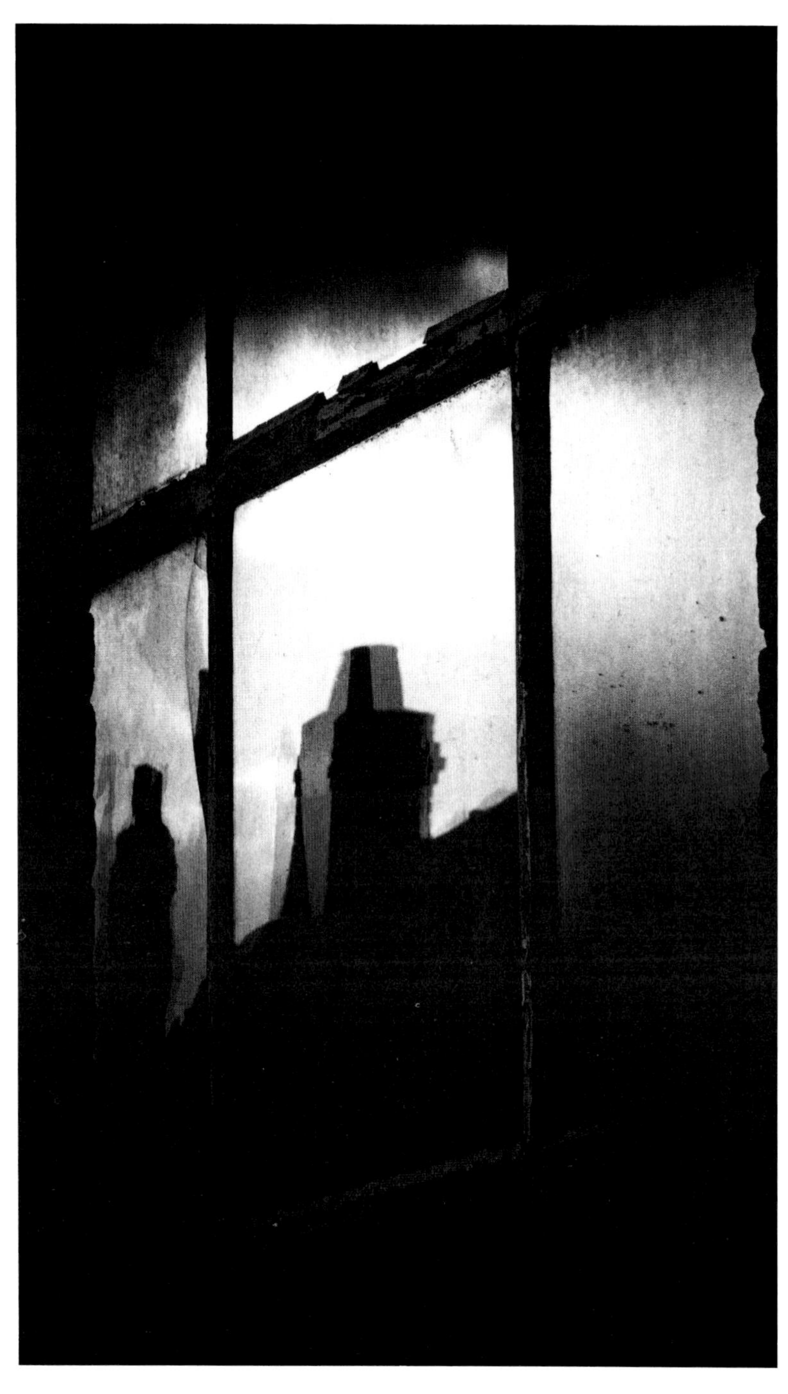

Old mill window
Oldham, Greater Manchester

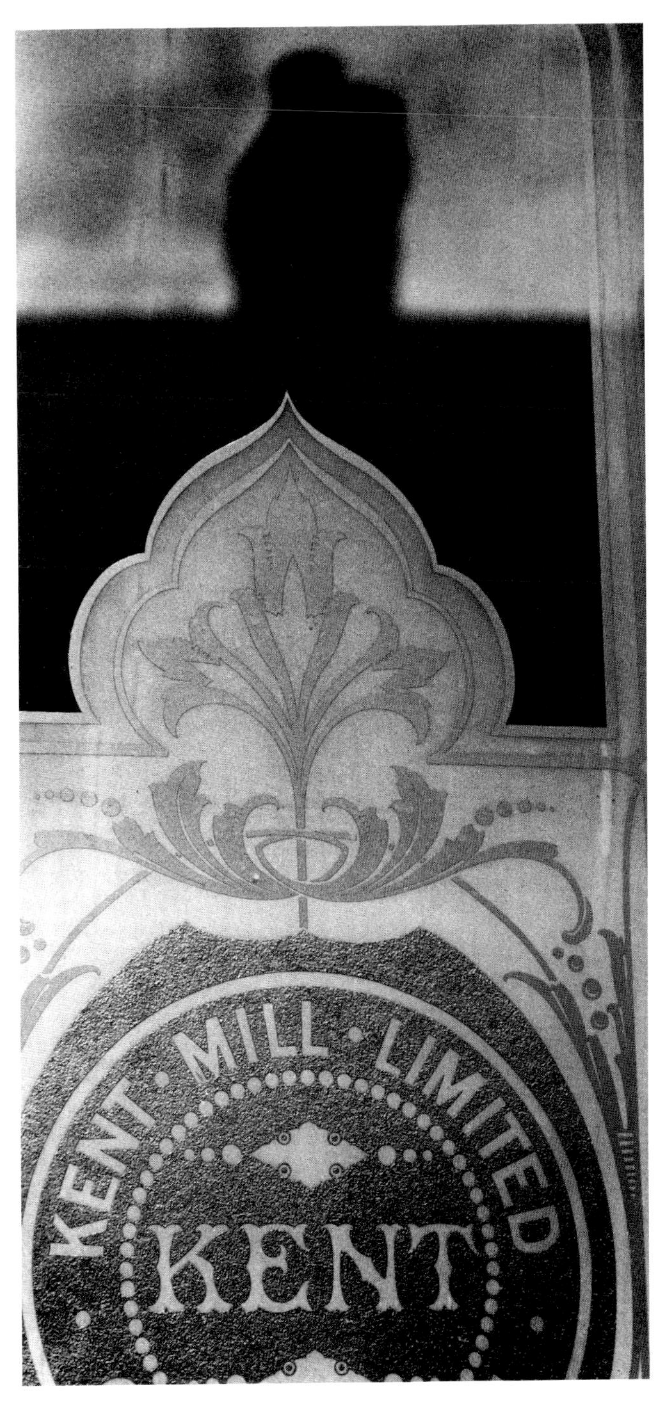

Etched-glass mill window
Chadderton, Greater Manchester

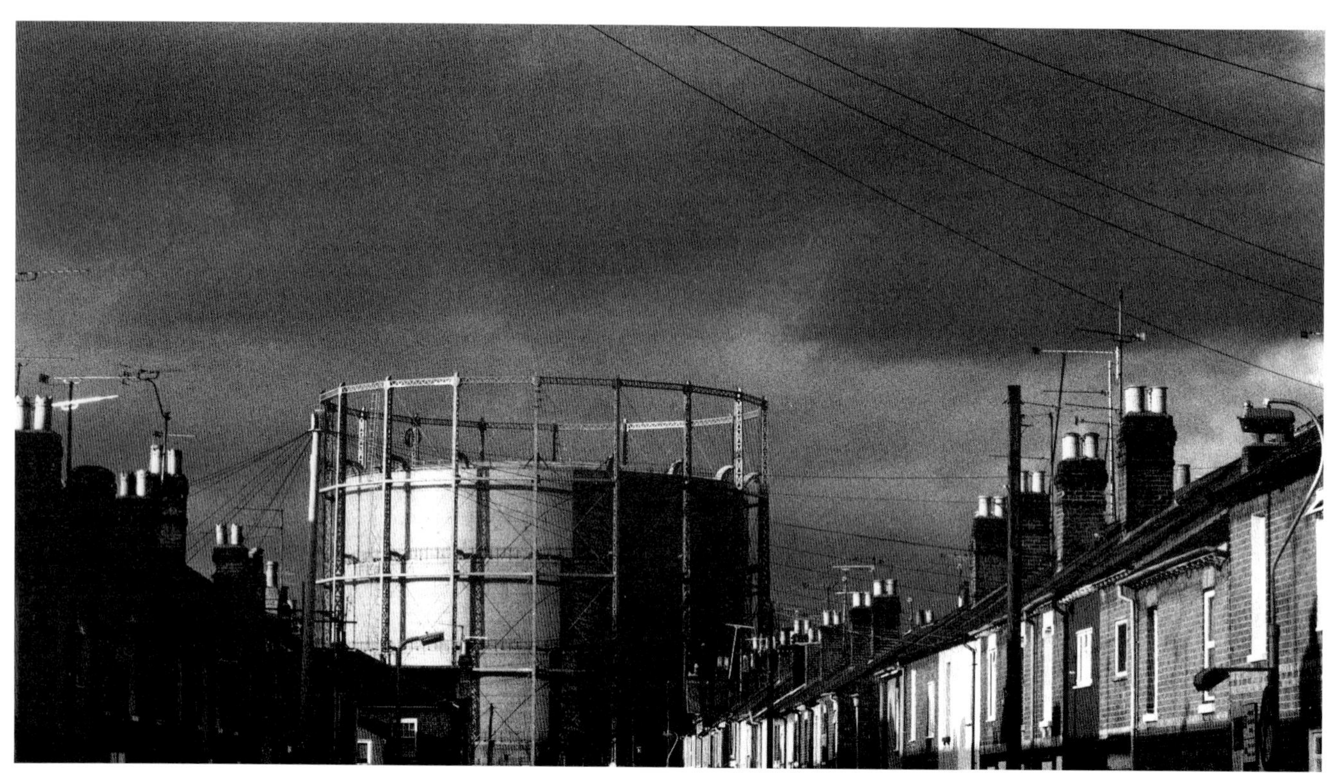

Cumberland Road, Reading

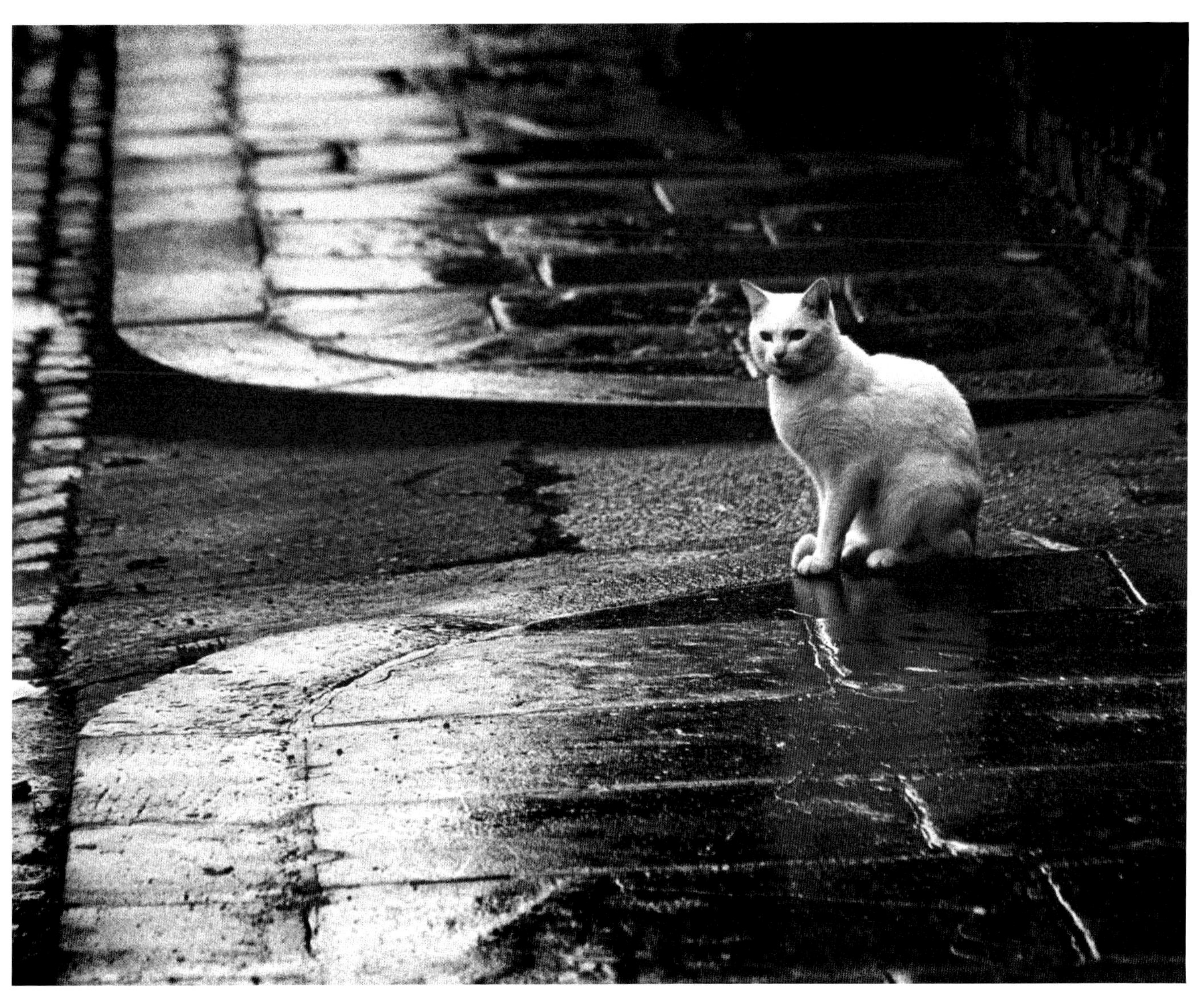

'White' moggy
Saltaire, West Yorkshire

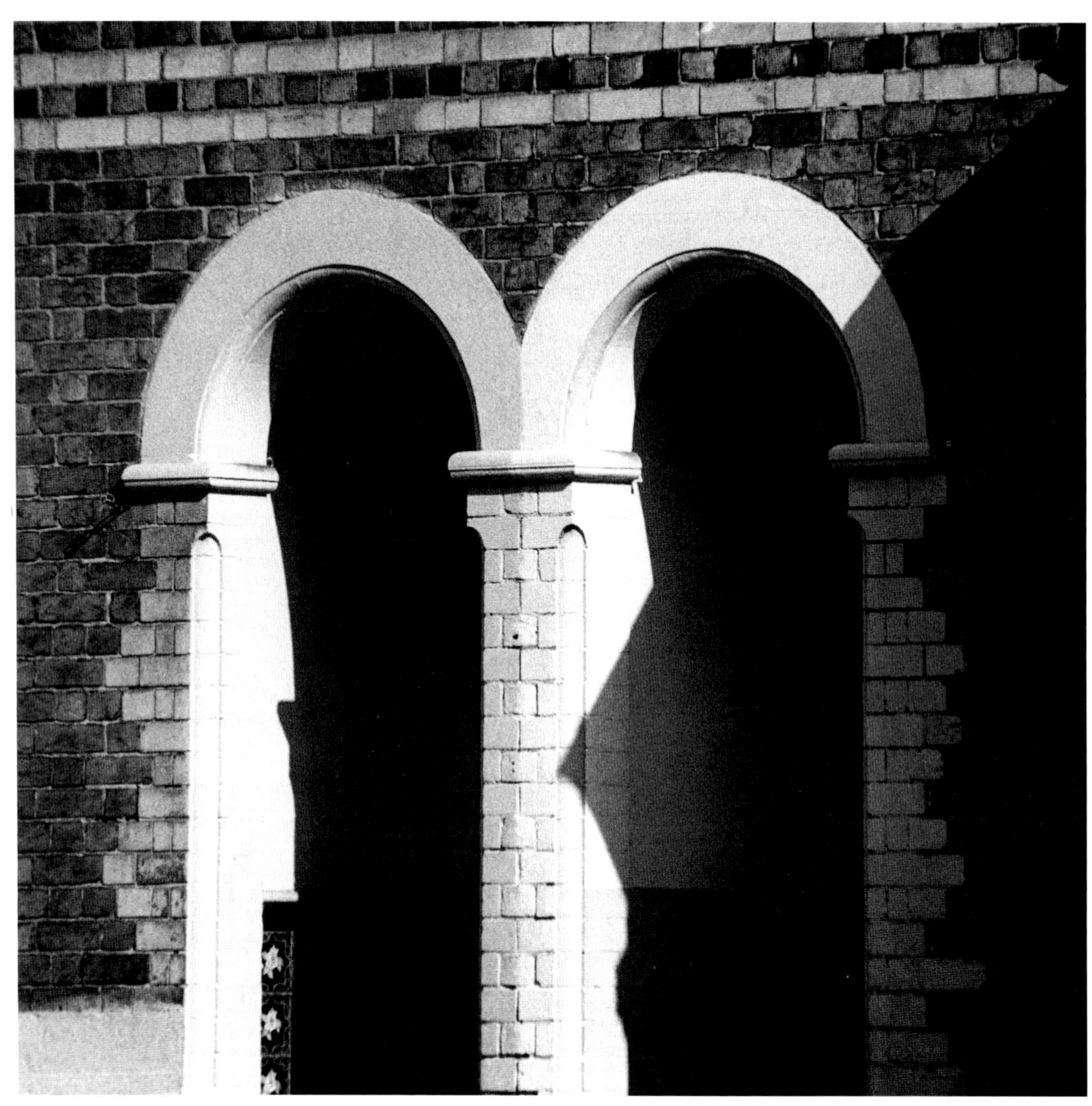

Doorways
Reading

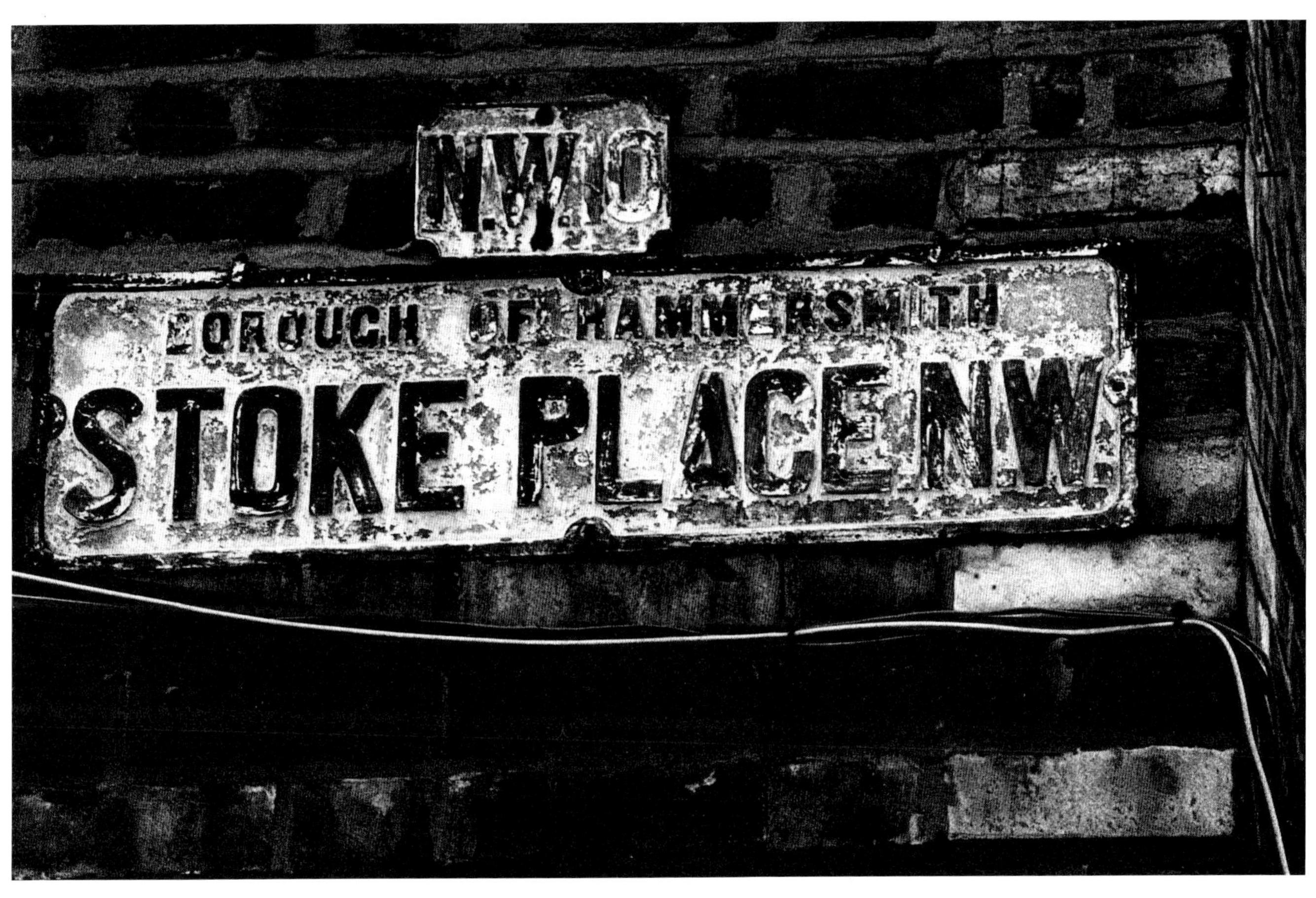

Road sign, Willesden

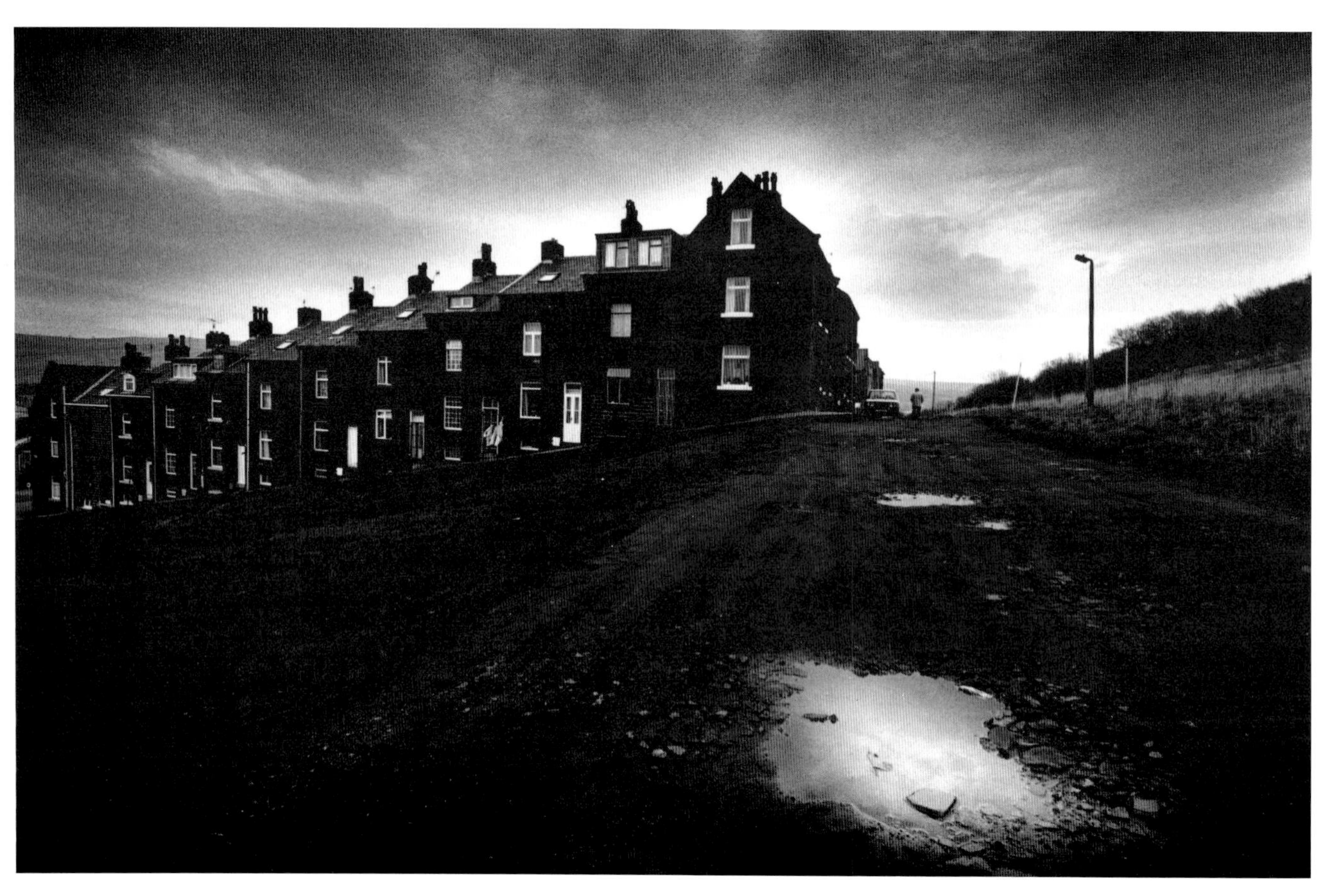

Keighley, Yorkshire

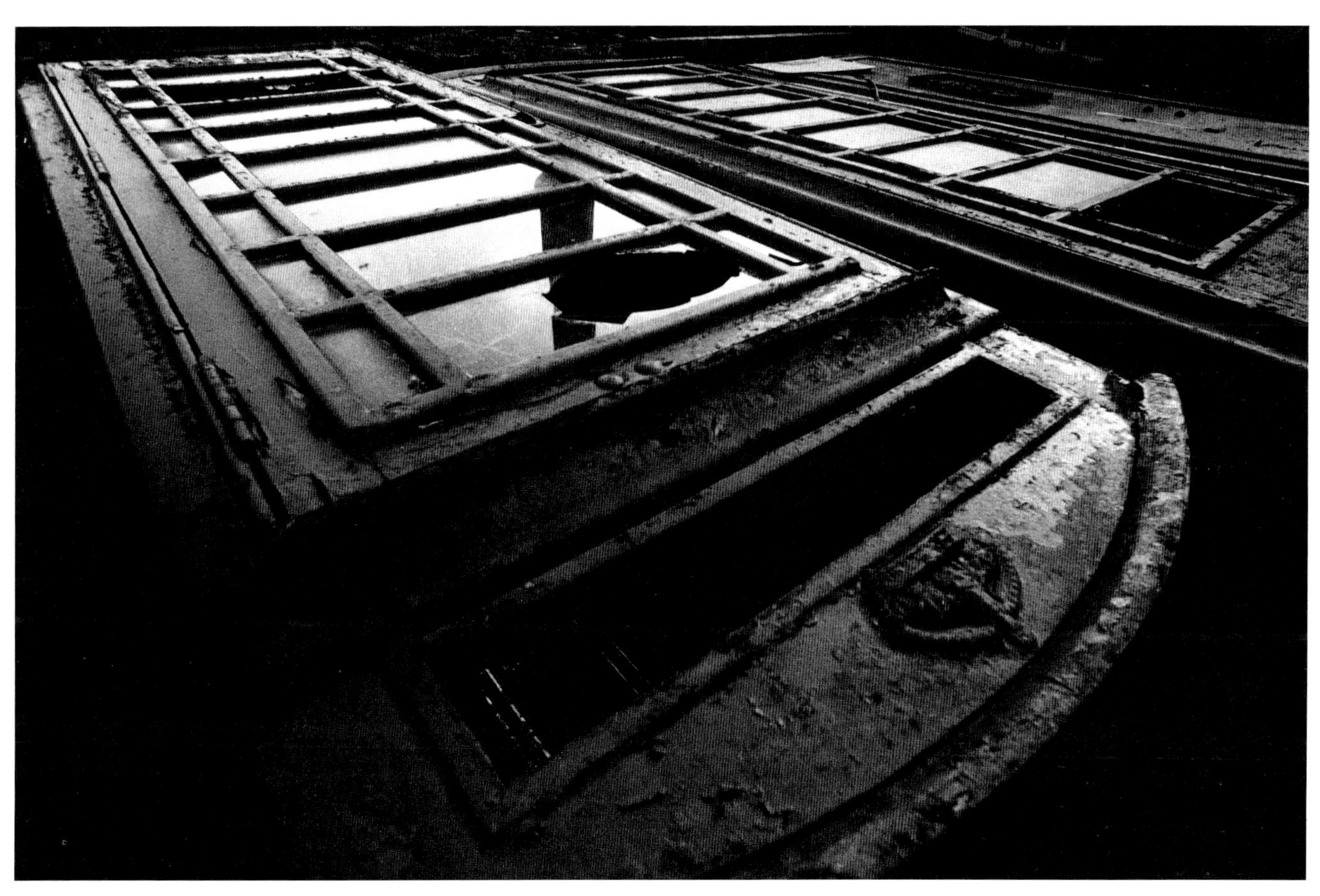

Old telephone boxes
Elland, Yorkshire

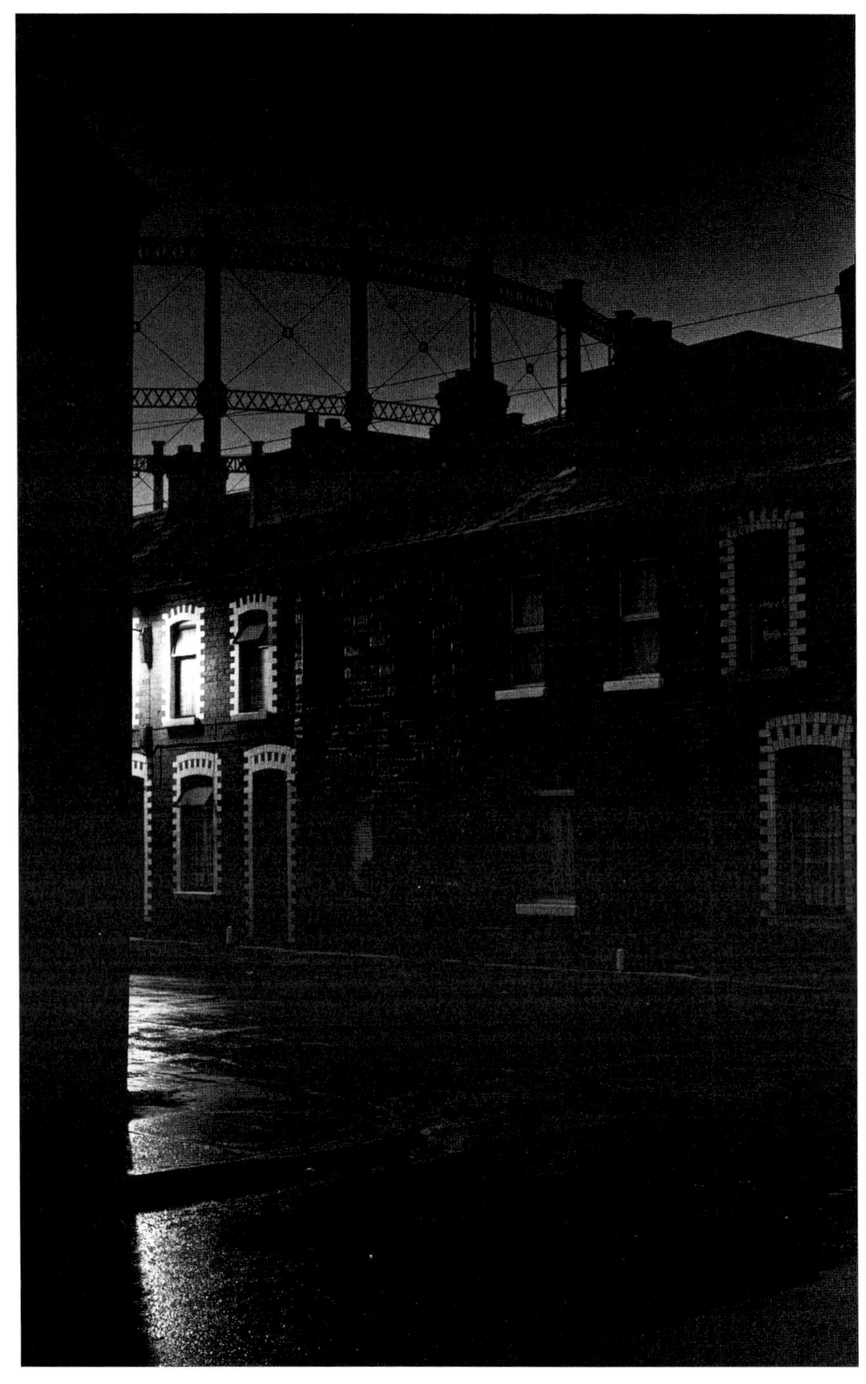

Urban night
Dublin, Ireland

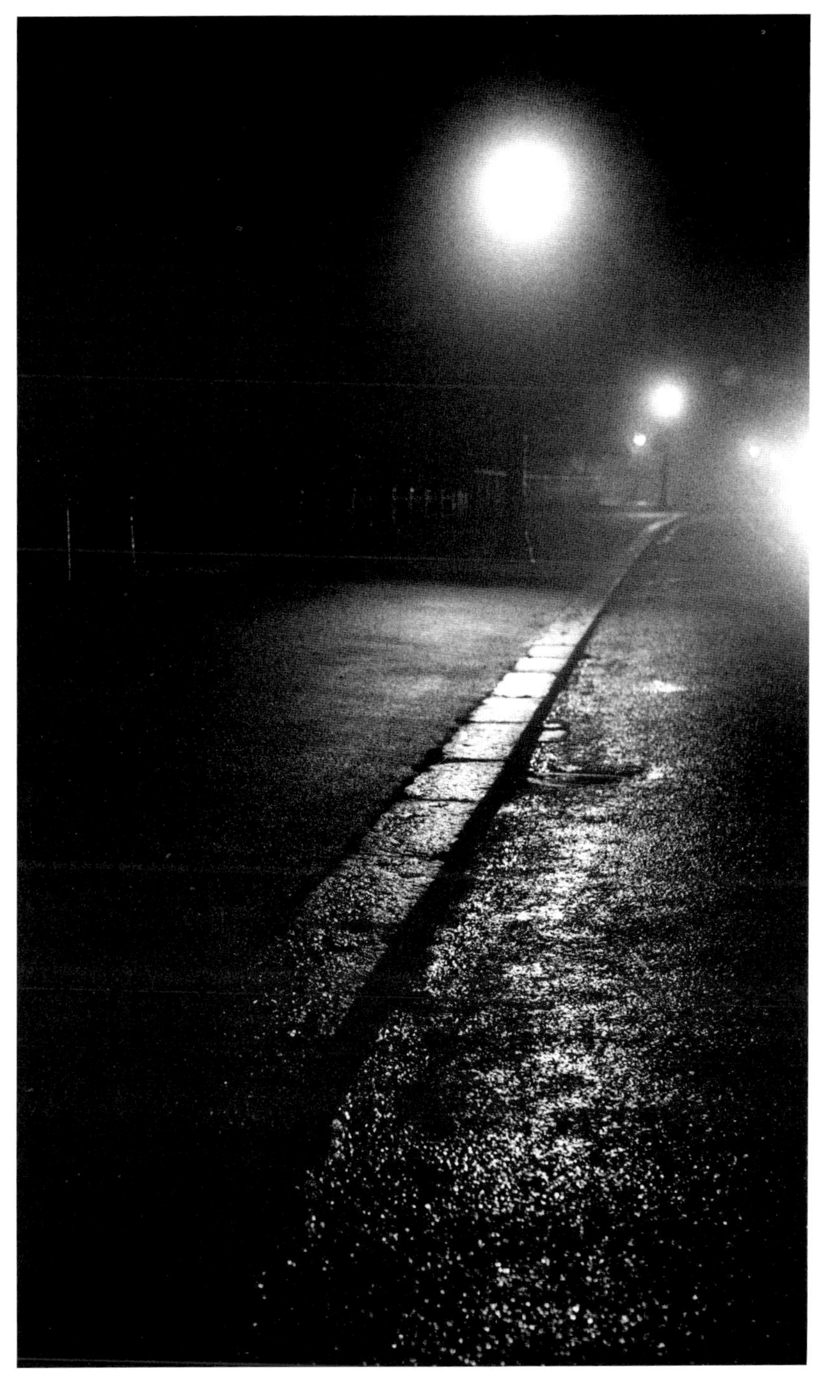

Gas lamps
Phoenix Park, Dublin

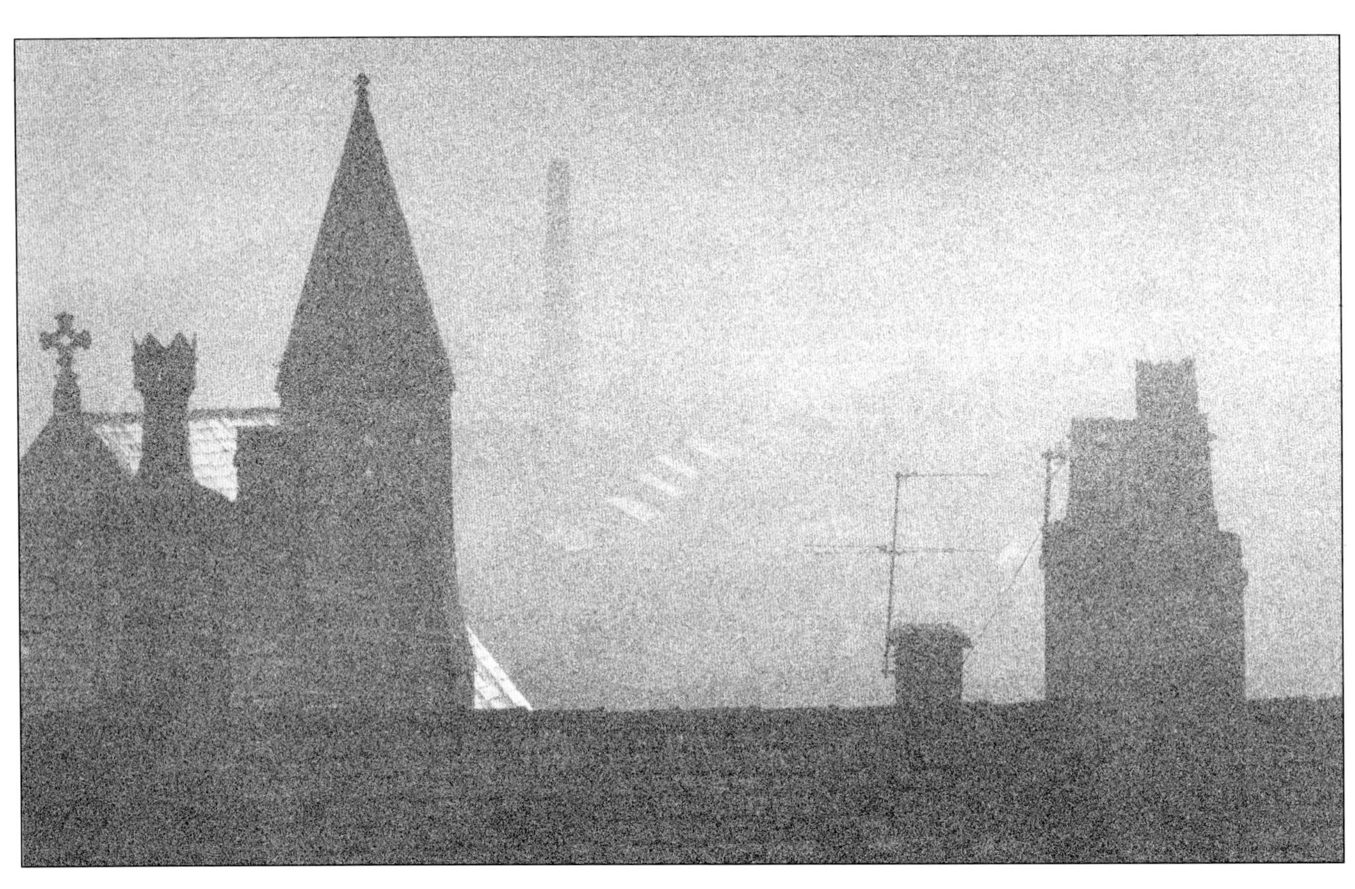

Autumn morning
Clitheroe, Lancashire

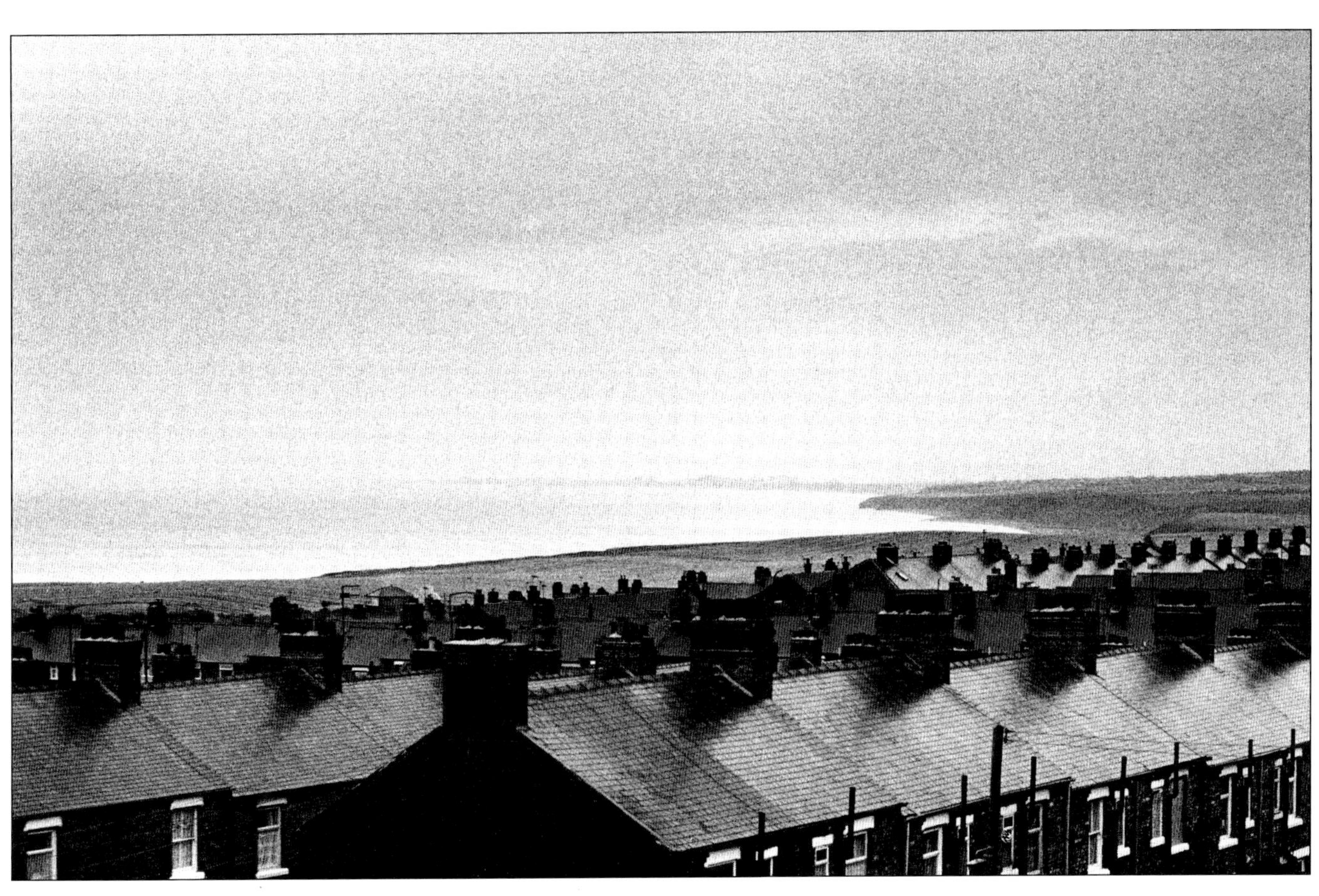

Easington colliery village
East Durham

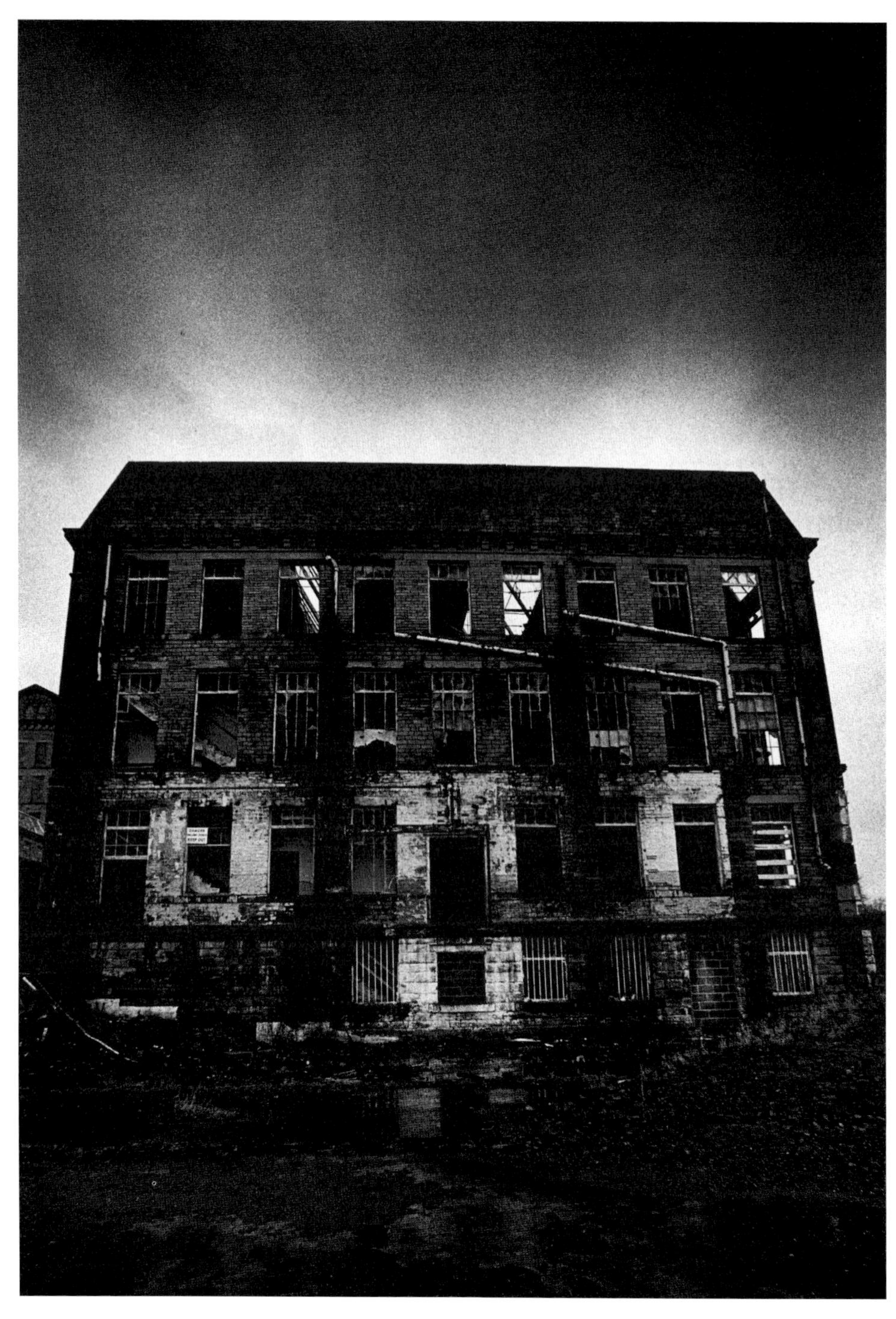

Derelict mill
Saltaire, West Yorkshire

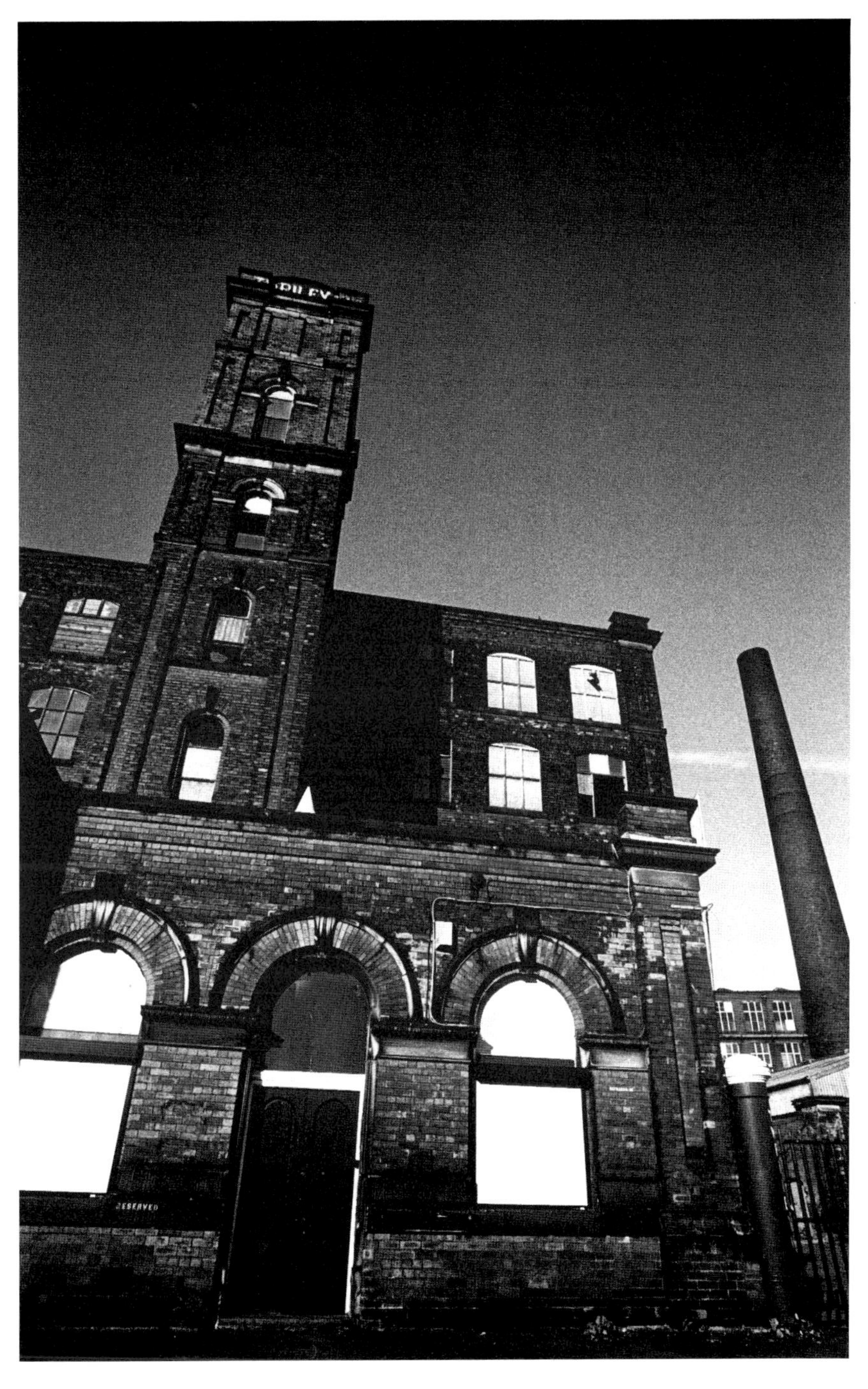

Derelict mill
Rochdale, Lancashire

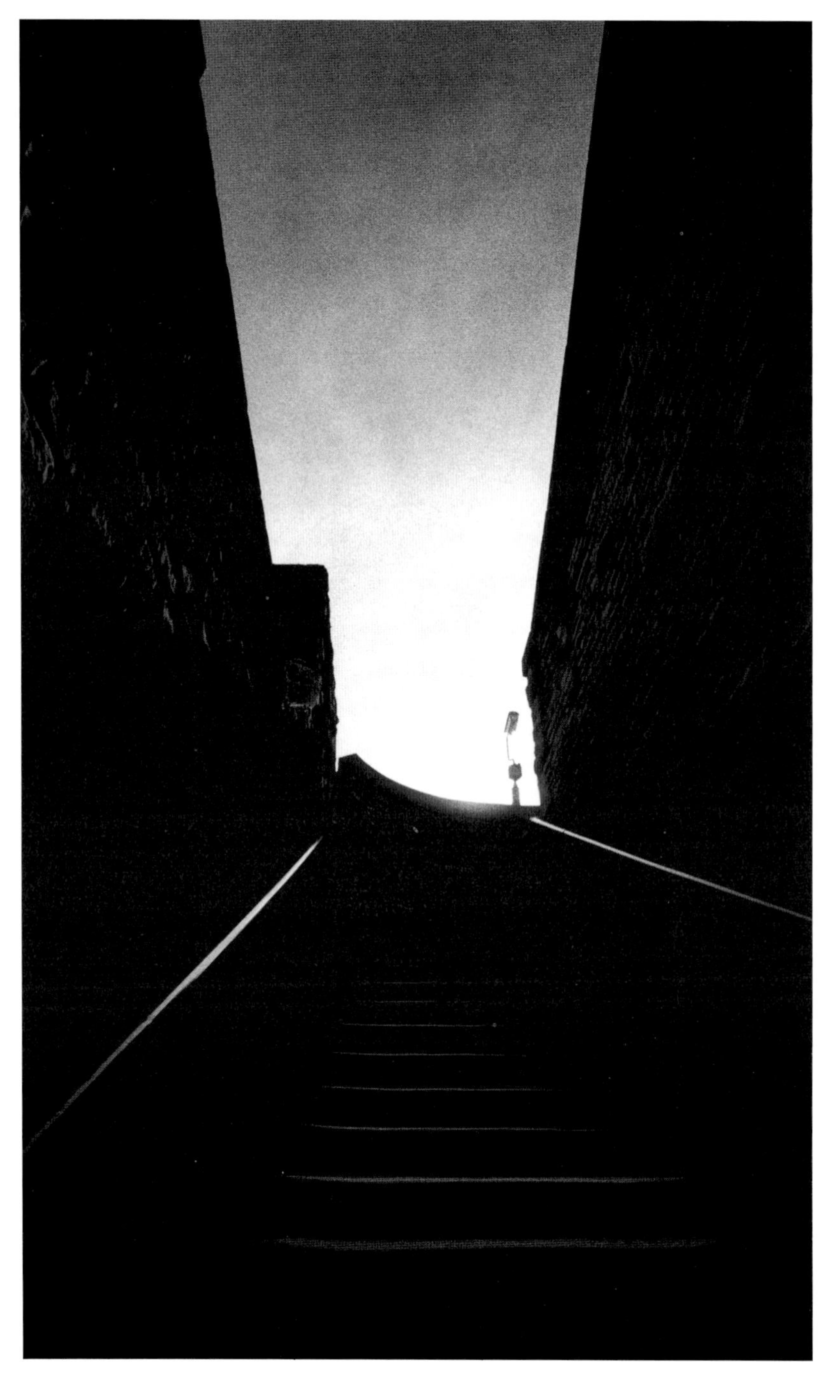

Subway
Halifax, Yorkshire

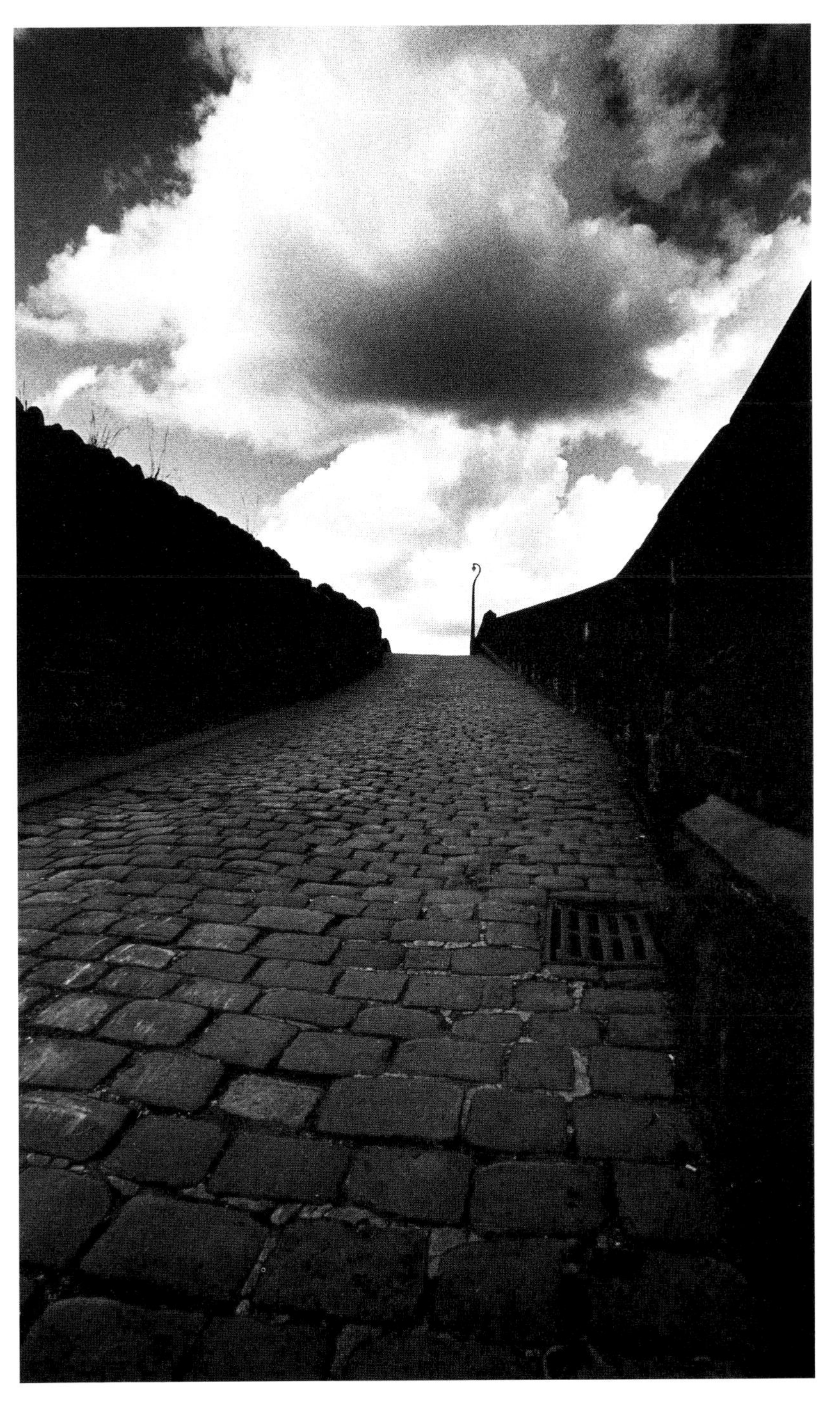

Cobbled roadway
Burnley, Lancashire

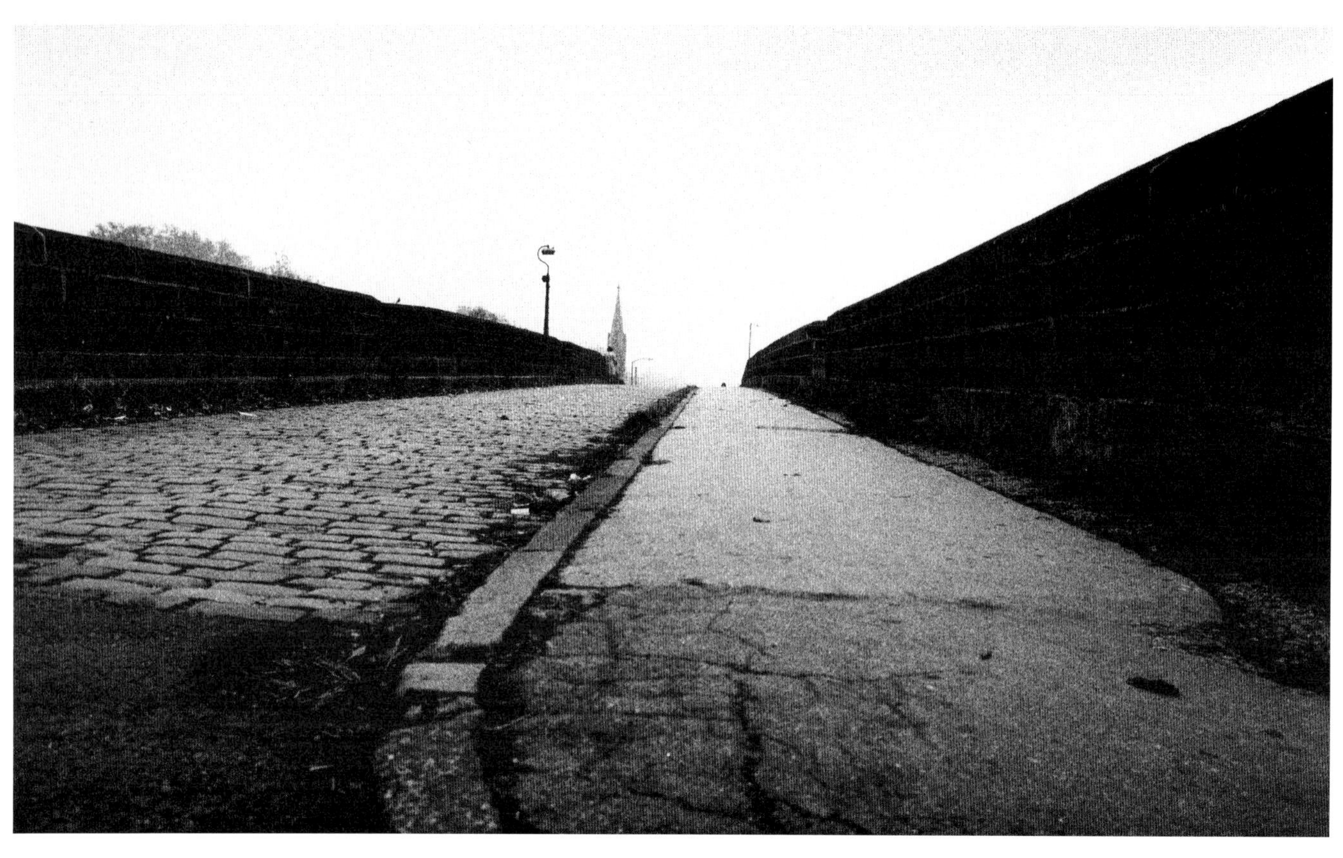

Penwortham Bridge
Preston, Lancashire

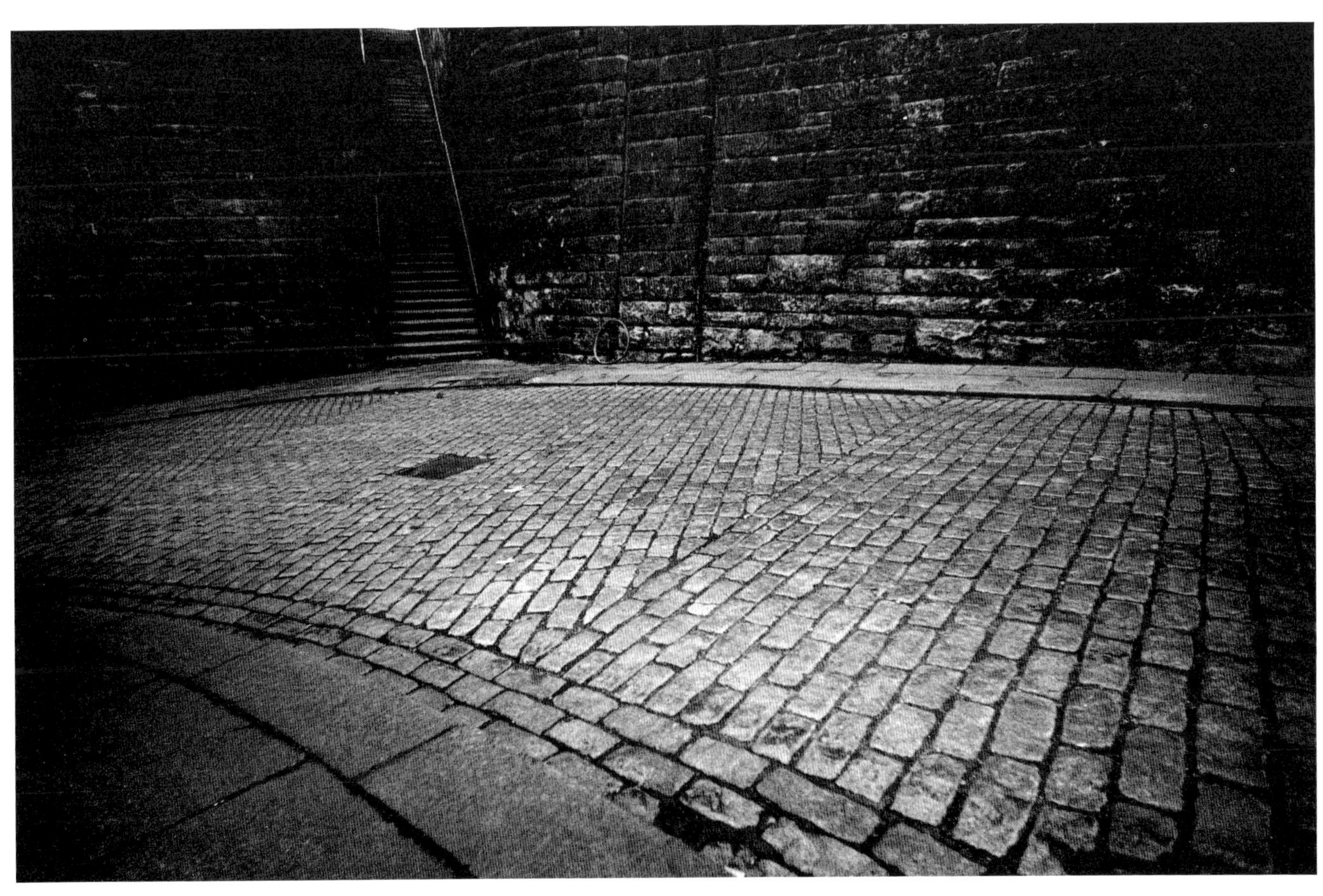

Scotswood, Newcastle

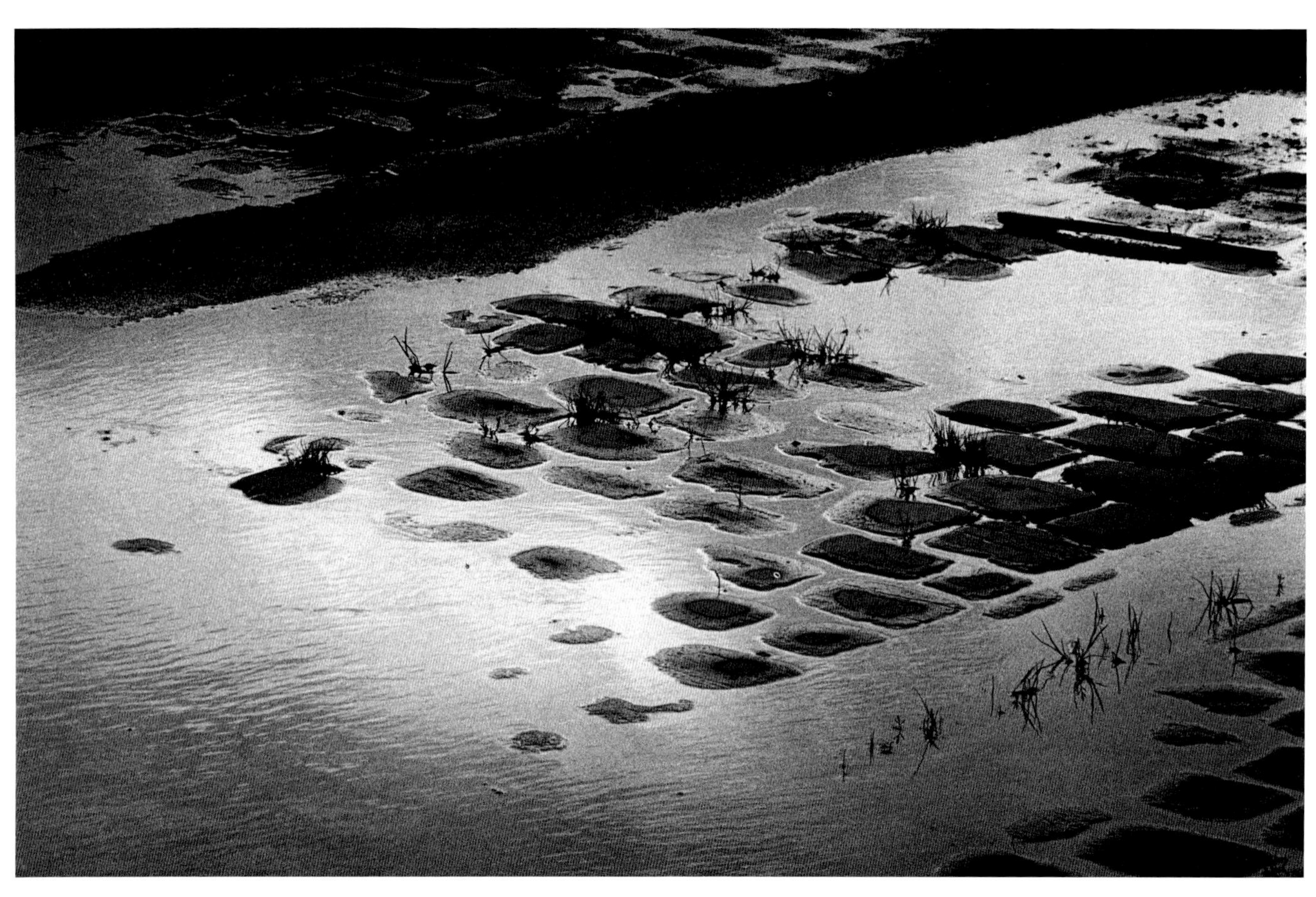

Cobbles and weeds
By the Manchester Ship Canal, Salford

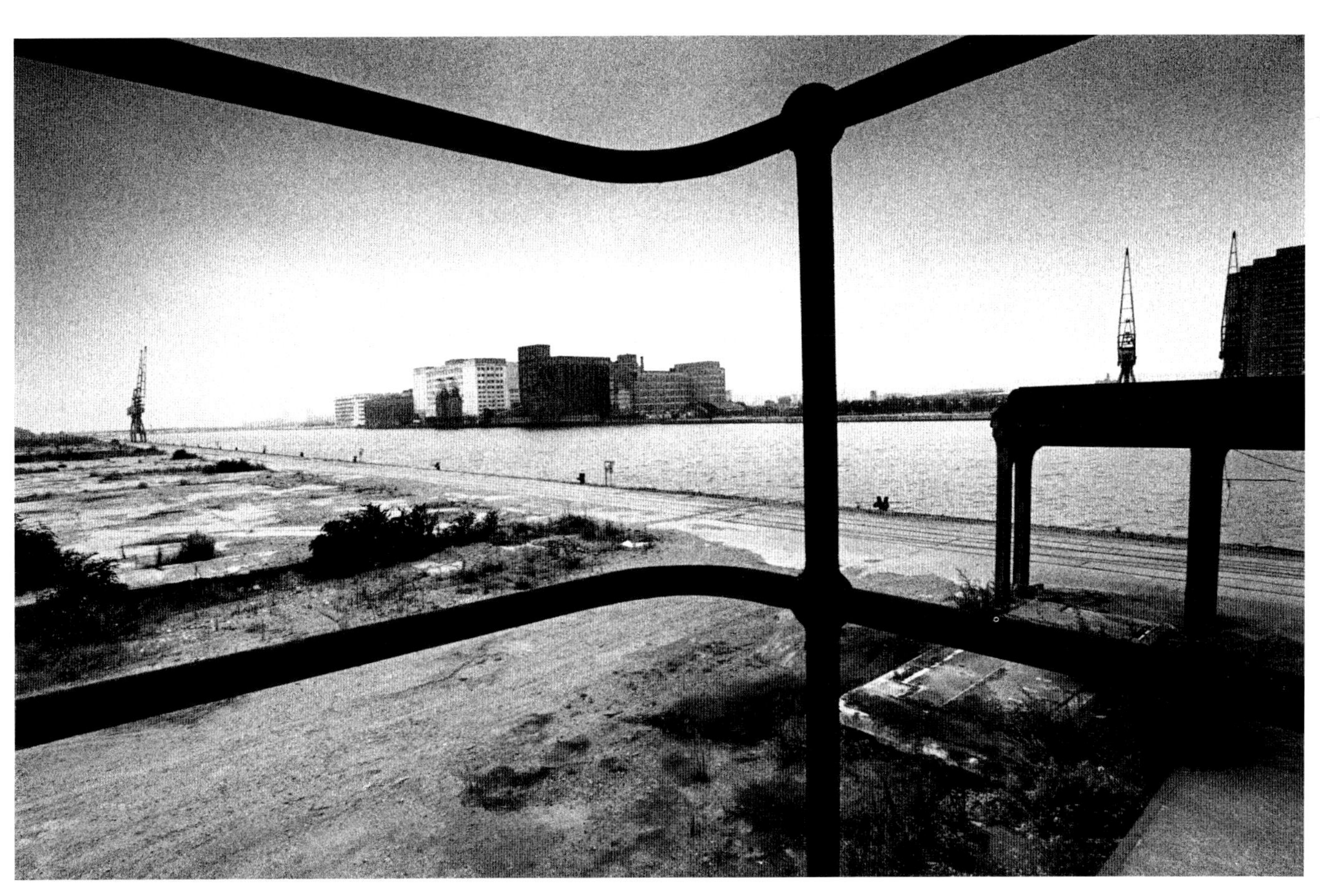

The Royal Docks, London

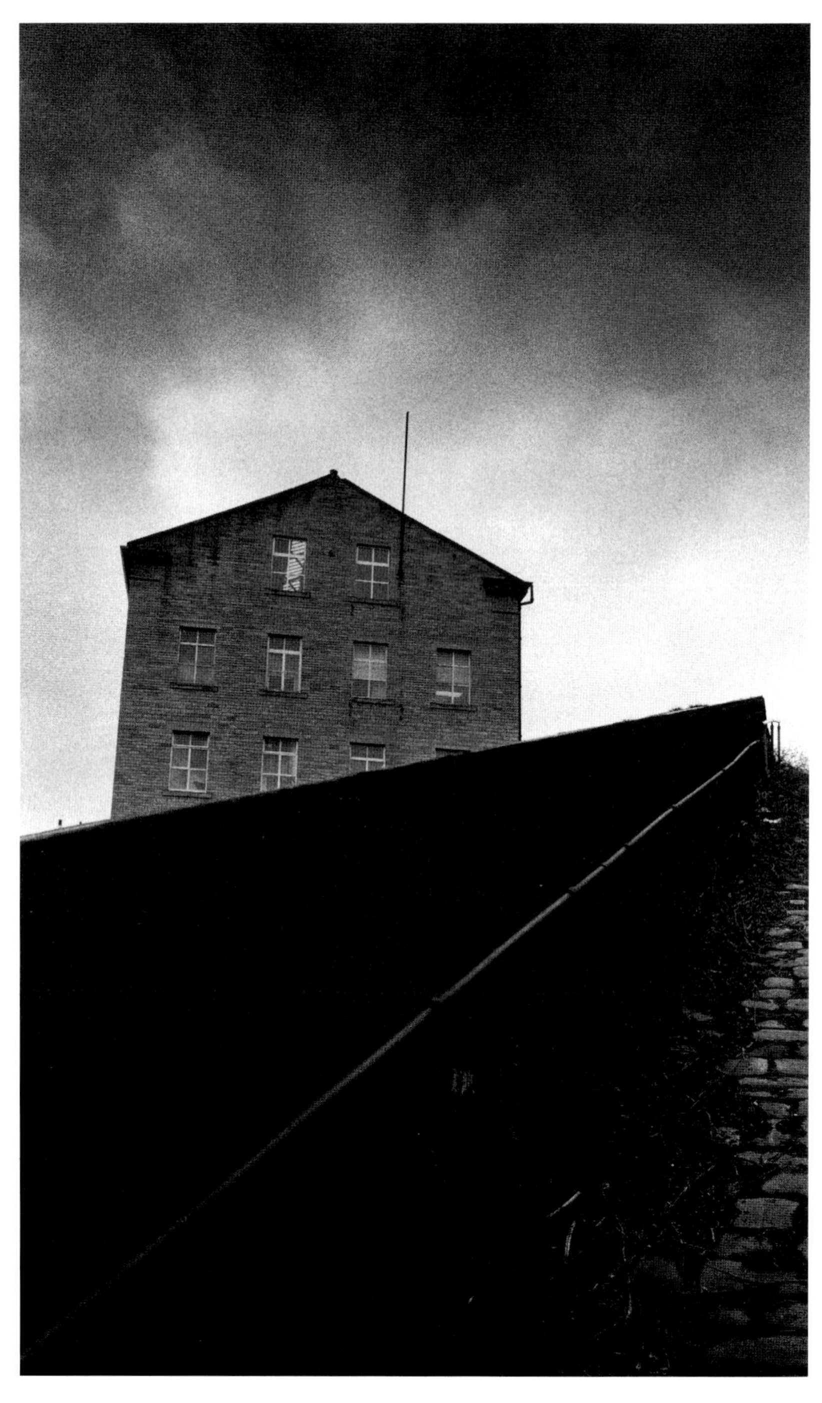

Bill Brandt's snicket
Halifax, Yorkshire

Why can't it stay like this forever
Why does it always have to change
Everytime you think you've paid the price
Seems you've always got to pay it twice
Everytime you think you're near the end
You turn around and find another ticket

Eric Clapton

Technical notes

For me, the image is more important than the techniques used to capture it. I have leant heavily on memory and early influences for the photographs in this book. However, I appreciate that some readers will want to know a little more on how I go about getting these images.

To find my subjects, I use Ordnance Survey 1:10,000 maps. I usually photograph in the early morning or late afternoon, generally photographing against the light, which I find helps to create the atmosphere I am seeking. I often photograph alone, walking miles in all weathers to find what I want.

Often the image forms in my mind long before I take the photographs: a sketch book comes in handy for ideas and notes that surface at 4am. The most difficult factor is trying to balance the imagination and the reality.

Details

Cameras:	Canon 35mm slr and lenses; Mamiya 645.
Film:	HP5, Tri-X, Agfapan 25 – all rated normally.
Paper:	Agfa Brovira Speed grade 4 or Ilford Multigrade.
Grain effect:	Contact positive grain screen.